From the Award winning author of the book
From Park Bench to Park Avenue

GHETTO PRACTITIONER

ANTHONY BROWN

SQUARE TREE PUBLISHING
www.SquareTreePublishing.com
Copyright © 2025 by Anthony Brown
For more information about bulk purchases, please contact Anthony Brown at info@anthonyhowardbrown.com.
Cover Design By: Humble Books
ISBN: 978-1-957293-72-1
Library of Congress Control Number: 2025911226

For Nancy Clark,
the woman who believed in me...

ACKNOWLEDGMENTS

I must give recognition to some people who have made the contents of this book possible. First, I must thank my mother, Jeanette Joan Saffold, for giving me the ability to experience life with all its nuances. A mother who inadvertently planted a seed while not understanding the exact nature of the soil but always having faith that from heaven the rain would eventually fall, and this flower would bloom.

I must acknowledge my dear friend Dr. Drew Pinsky. I now know in life, darkness comes before the storm. In my journey, you have shown me that no matter how cloudy the skies are, we can always stay dry as long as we remember to open the umbrella. You once told me that my outside reality is cheated by my inner thoughts. This simple statement is profound and so true. With this book, I want to say, "Here I am again, dear doctor," taking another step forward, just as you encouraged. I fully grasp that life is not about the destination, but about enjoying the many fruits I discover while on this journey.

For the many supervisors who saw something in me that I haven't yet discovered in myself, I thank you: George, you challenged me; Donna, you believed in me; and Victoria, you tolerated me as I learned more about my craft. You three have gifted me with the fine art of discovering something useful to benefit those I can serve. With enduring patience, you all have supported me as I faced some challenging times throughout my employment career. Your belief in me created confidence that matured into courage and strength when navigating difficult situations with complex people.

I must give thanks to my direct nursing staff: Mae, Kitzy, and Nellie. You three have endured my multiple mood swings, implemented new ideas, and provided close support to the clients we were blessed to serve. I owe you all a big thank you for walking through the rain alongside me during this journey.

I want to give thanks to many individuals and entities who either supported or rejected my first book, *From Park Bench to Park Avenue*. Your kind words, along with your critical reviews, have given me the courage and strength to be brave once again. Even the negative feedback I received was the thunder that forced me to get out of the weather and find the means to stay safe.

I give thanks to Debbie Martin for the late-night conversations we shared, and the support you provided in teaching me the importance of family dynamics. You are truly the rainbow that I look forward to on the horizon.

Of course, I thank God for His omnipotence and omnipresence in my life. Without His hand, I would not have made this journey.

Lastly, I thank Sparrow (Woodstock), whose smile is the beacon that guides my journey. My fellow traveler who wasn't afraid of getting her feet wet.

I often tell people I talk with God daily, and He responds to me. One day, a friend asked what God's voice sounded like. I had to think about it and did not have an answer, but I told him I would ask God Himself. I went home, prayed with the question in mind, and received an answer. I went back to my friend and said, "I asked God about your question, and He gave me an answer for you." Curious, my friend asked what the reply was. The answer was simply this…

"God told me to tell you He uses sign language and that all you must do is watch what I do, and you will see."

TABLE OF CONTENTS

FOREWORD

Anthony Brown knows. He knows because he has been there. He lived for years as a homeless addict, existing by trafficking drugs. Anthony knows because he survived severe childhood trauma and, with resilience, started down the long road of recovery and never looked back.

Anthony knows because he became an extraordinary professional, a nurse, who now serves those who themselves suffer homelessness, addiction, and mental illness.

And here Anthony provides us with a continuation of his story, his work for those enduring the plight of homelessness and trauma, admonishing us all to remind ourselves that every human deserves dignity and freedom from stereotyping. The stigma around homelessness only serves to inflame it. Anthony reminds us to reach out. Contact is the only sure remedy for stigma. And contact may be the one intervention that turns someone's life around. Brains change other brains, and Anthony reminds us further that community and connection heals. No one chooses to be homeless any more than someone chooses to be an addict. A combination of factors conspires to create the road to homelessness, which is littered with common brain conditions and the consequence of trauma and adverse childhood experiences.

In *The Ghetto Practitioner*, Anthony reveals that life is filled with challenges; scaling one mountain may reveal others we must climb in the distance. We must practice putting one foot in front of the other, daily. But once again, this walking miracle man reminds us that life can be a celebration, a life of meaning and thriving. Anthony knows, because he, but for the Grace of God, has walked in the shoes of those who suffer, and he has recovered to help those he hopes to lift up.

Dr. Drew Pinsky, MD

INTRODUCTION

Most people desire to accomplish many things. Some want to be homeowners, nurses, travelers exploring new places. Others long to be change-makers, advocates for the less fortunate, educators, or media influencers. Some aspire to earn graduate degrees, write books, or believe in something greater—to do something long-lasting beyond this world. But why do only a few ever reach their goals? I have always wondered this, because these dreams are within the reach of all of us. After all, I have done all this, despite starting out in life with a statistically unfavorable chance of doing any of them. Trauma, pain, addiction and homelessness left me facing life with only an eighth-grade education. The secret to reaching these goals wasn't hard to figure out: time, perseverance, education, and faith—lots of faith—as well as the willingness to surrender and do the work you need to do for yourself.

I have discovered that the best way to navigate life is to be mildly eccentric! To ask the "dumb questions," for with every question comes answers. *The Ghetto Practitioner*, the follow-up to my memoir, *From Park Bench to Park Avenue*, is my journey of coming to the end of one path, and into the beginning of yet another ending.

Every beginning must come to an end, and every end starts a new beginning. "Life gets lifey" as my friend Haley says, and nothing worthwhile comes easy. We are not good at most things in the beginning and feel uncoordinated while we learn. There is truth to that. At times, I feel like I am "so ghetto" at practicing this life of faith. And that is where this book finds me—once again facing monsters and demons. But this time, they are not of my own making but what life has thrown at me. After the surprising success of *Park Bench,* change and opportunity to finish some amazing dreams began—one of them being the Brown Manor recovery home. The move back to my home state, appearing regularly on HSBN media, and an unexpected diagnosis all helped me refocus once again on my purpose here on this planet. Once you think you have things all figured out, you realize there is more work to do. Practice never truly makes perfect, but it keeps you relying on your beliefs when everything turns upside down.

As with all life, once we are created, the clock starts ticking toward the end. There is no stopping that train. So, let's ride it together, hang tight to God through the bumps, and take this road of Happy Destiny. And always remember: "Life is groovy."

Chapter One
DAZED

Dreaming

I once dreamed of being homeless. I tried to run, but my feet wouldn't move. My arms felt cold, and a hand grabbed my shirt, twisting and tightening it around my arm. I saw the broken, dirty fingernails and filthy clothes—signs of the life I thought I'd left behind. My arm ached as the blood dripped down my forearm. When the pain hit, I realized the truth—I had relapsed. A streetlight flickered, illuminating the intersection of Harbor and Wilson. No one was there but me—alone, ashamed, undone. Warm tears stung my cheeks as I whispered, "What have I done, Lord?" The guilt suffocated me. I hated myself for falling again. But in that moment of despair, I felt something holy whisper: *"I'm still here."* I woke up trembling, heart racing, drenched in sweat. My thoughts grasped for what was real. It was a nightmare of regret and guilt. I contemplated that moment, wondering, *will I ever end up there again?*

Thank God those days are behind me. Today, my life is marked by gratitude. I sit at my favorite spot—the dining room table—surrounded by tranquility, writing and studying with a thankful heart. Beside me sits Bunny, my little stuffed blue rabbit, quietly keeping watch—a gentle reminder of how far I've come.

Also on my table sits my favorite coffee cup, the one with Winnie the Pooh smiling just above the rim, arms crossed in playful delight. The aroma rising from it changes as the day goes on: Folgers coffee in the morning and a rotating selection of teas at night. Whatever fills the cup, it rarely stays warm; once I begin writing, I drift into a dreamlike creative state where time slips away. Beside it rests my Bible—the same one I discovered years ago while incarcerated—a quiet, constant presence that grounds me. Together, these familiar items create the sacred space where this story was born. But before we step into the journey ahead, let me share a bit about who I am—or, perhaps more truthfully, who I used to be.

I came from a difficult and unstable childhood. Raised by a single mother, alongside two sisters and a brother, I was the second youngest—often wearing hand-me-downs that never quite fit, too short in some places, too long in others. I ran away in my early teens and survived by working as a "carnie" in a traveling carnival until I was eighteen. I never made it past the eighth grade as addiction quickly took its place, and my years were lost to drugs and alcohol. I found recovery at thirty-seven, and since that moment, I haven't touched a drink or illegal substance. Between 1992 and 2001, I spent much of my life incarcerated—caught in a cycle of release, relapse, and rearrest, never free for more than a few months at a time. Today, I have lived in recovery for over twenty years. I have earned a master's degree in nursing, written a book, and been interviewed on television networks across the U.S., the U.K., and Australia. I have both dined with celebrities and eaten free food from soup kitchens. I guess you could say I have had a well-rounded life.

Heroes

Most of us grow up with childhood dreams, with images of heroes who shape the person we long to become. For me, my role model wasn't a typical one. It was Fred G. Sanford from the 1970s sitcom *Sanford and Son*. Something about his sharp wit and hustle stuck with me. I used to imagine what it might be like to "mix champagne with cheap wine," a phrase that somehow captured the chaos and longing in my life. I didn't have many real-life figures to look up to. Most of my early years weren't about dreaming, but about surviving.

I didn't truly understand what a real hero was until much later in life. I found him somewhere in the first five years of my sobriety—not out in the world, but within me. Now in recovery, I began to see myself through a different lens—one shaped by truth, growth, and grace.

Today, my story has completely changed.

I had been in prison for about a year when I discovered a way to connect with God. After my release, I connected with Him directly. That connection was so profound that, even to this day, it still resonates within me. This process unfolded slowly as I moved from questioning the existence of God to walking hand-in-hand with my Creator. My life is now fully committed to practicing what I discovered many years ago. Not all events in life are wonderful, but every one of them was worth living. I am dazed in the light of life's goodness. Sometimes, I literally want to pinch myself, just to make sure that this is all real and not some crazy dream.

Harbor and Wilson

It isn't hard for me to remember when the change first began. Living on the streets of Costa Mesa, California, and daily using a lot of methamphetamine, cocaine, and alcohol, I had burned every bridge with anyone who might have helped me. At thirty-five, I was reduced to a hopeless state—both physically and mentally. I didn't shower regularly, mostly because of guilt and shame. I was angry all the time—not necessarily at others, but at myself. I had no real coping skills and refused to let anyone tell me what to do. I was a lost soul, never even considering that I could be saved. In those days, I always seemed to end up at the intersection of Harbor and Wilson, where, even now, the same old Jack-in-the-Box I once worked at still stands, a silent witness to that dark chapter of my life.

That intersection was where so much of my life played out, something many of you may already know. Heavily addicted to drugs, cycling in and out of prisons, barely scraping by with just enough common sense to fill a Dixie cup. Then one day, Officer McCollough from the Costa Mesa Police Department asked if I wanted help. I guess he could tell that I was in dire straits. I was physically, mentally, emotionally, and spiritually bankrupt. Something inside me finally spoke up, and I said, "Yes, I need help." And that moment marked the beginning of my journey.

Nancy Clark and Jill Hubbard are the first names that come to mind when I think back to that time. I remember the day I first met them—they introduced me to a place that offered me my first real chance at normality. It was an apartment complex called The Recovery Center, and within that environment, I learned what it meant to be a productive member of society. With the guidance of those counselors and the unwavering support of my close friend, Marnie Tucker, I broke free from the chains of childhood trauma and began my metamorphosis into the person I am today. Countless others played a role in that transformation, and many of them are familiar to you if you've read my first book.

As I take another sip of coffee, the memories of those days resurface, and I can't help but reflect on the stark contrast between the Anthony Brown of Costa Mesa and the Anthony Brown of Mansfield.

Working

Though my intentions were sincere, those early days were filled with obstacles. Finding a job as a convicted felon with no recent work history was incredibly difficult. Aside from my time as a carnie, I had little to offer on a résumé. My first real adult job was in telemarketing—a tough position for someone already battling deep feelings of rejection. Most people didn't want what I was selling, and they made that painfully clear. Still, I was determined to change, and moving backward wasn't an option. But without real coping skills, I eventually gave up and relapsed, finding myself with a return ticket to prison. It was a setback, but something had taken root. A seed had been planted. And when I was released, I was determined to give "normal" life another shot.

I stayed sober and found a new job as a house manager at a sober living facility. Dave, a counselor from The Recovery Center, introduced me to Lynda Klinger, who worked at a respected treatment center in Tustin called Cornerstone. That connection opened the door to a new opportunity—working in the office—and eventually inspired me to return to school. Cornerstone became the catalyst for my future in recovery. I had earned my GED while in jail, and though that was the extent of my formal education at the time, I took a leap and enrolled in college in 2001, all while continuing to work at Cornerstone.

Second Chances

I am a firm believer in second chances. I have been given more than my share. Nancy Clark offered me a second chance at life;

the education system gave me a second chance to learn; and society gave me a second chance to contribute, through employers who took a risk on me. And above all, God has given me countless second chances, more than I deserve, and still does. That kind of grace changed me. It taught me to extend the same to others. As my good friend Nate Tarango often reminds me, "Don't forget where you come from." That simple truth has become a guiding principle in my life and one I plan to carry with me to the very end.

The past is part of me, and forgetting it can be dangerous. What is forgotten is often repeated. That truth keeps me grounded. And with all I've accomplished, I never take my current life for granted, because under the wrong circumstances, I could find myself back on a park bench some day. Only the Lord knows whether life would offer me yet another do-over. But that awareness keeps me humble and walking forward with gratitude.

My job at Cornerstone became the stepping stone to a series of opportunities in the nursing field. From there, I moved on to Fairview Developmental Center, then to West Anaheim Extended Care, followed by Westminster Extended Care. I'm still pursuing coursework in nursing today, continuing to grow in the field. Eventually, I even found myself teaching at Cypress College. It just goes to show that embracing second chances can lead to truly unexpected and meaningful places.

The Ghetto Practitioner

Teacher

When I was first being considered for a full-time faculty position at the college, I had already made it through the interview rounds, cleared the background checks, and landed in the final pool of candidates. You'd think I would've felt confident, but a wave of anxiety rose inside me. Before that final interview, self-doubt hit hard. Thoughts telling me that I wasn't smart enough, wasn't good enough to be a college teacher. Sure, I had been a nurse for a while, but teaching at a community college felt like a whole different arena. Outwardly, I looked the part, dressed to the nines in a sharp white shirt with a starched collar, neatly tucked into pressed black slacks, and spit-shined black loafers. I looked good, no doubt about it. But inside, my thoughts told a different story. I kept thinking, *I'm a recovering alcoholic and addict. I'm not like the others. They have polished, academic lives. I barely scraped by with C's—how could I ever belong here?* Yes, my head was out to get me again, becoming my worst enemy, sabotaging me before the biggest interview of my life.

To calm the storm brewing within me, I stopped by The Friendship Club, a space where people in recovery can connect and breathe. I needed to chill out and gather myself. That's when I saw my friend Tammy B., someone I deeply respect, sitting quietly across the room. She looked up, gave me a nod, and in that small gesture, I felt a little steadier. Then, out of nowhere, she shouted across the room, "You got the wrong socks on!"

That unexpected burst of humor pulled me out of my head and back to earth, breaking the tension. I laughed, and fear lost its grip. It was a reminder not to take myself too seriously, that maybe, just maybe, I belonged more than I thought.

I went home, swapped out my white gym socks for a proper pair of black dress socks, and headed to the interview. I passed it that day and eventually got hired. Even now, I can't help but smile when I think back on it. Funny how some of life's most lasting lessons come from the most unexpected places.

COVID

Mortality has a way of sharpening my faith. I think I have this faith walk figured out, but in one crazy moment, I see how "ghetto" I am at believing God is in control. I question not just myself, but the work God places in front of me. While teaching at Cypress College, I also worked a second job at Westminster Therapeutic Residential Center. That's when COVID-19 hit. By March 2020, a national emergency was declared, and just like that, everything shifted. Life and faith became more real and present and more important to me than anything else.

It's something you don't easily forget once you've been through it, especially for those of us nurses, doctors, and frontline workers in healthcare during that time. The constant worry of whether you could go home after your shift because you sneezed or coughed, or receiving the news that you were infected and had to quarantine in a hotel. I vividly remember the staff shortages, running out of medical supplies, and trying to grasp patience with both hands, even when it felt impossible. The virus itself was tragic and stressful, but somehow, sanity had to be preserved.

Humor became my lifeline during those months. Keeping the team calm was a priority, so I dished out jokes like my friend Pat Leborio during one of his stand-up shows. I told friends that if the toilet paper shortage got any worse, I would dig a small hole in my yard take care of business, then cover it with dirt and plant a flower. I would call it "Rosey!" For toilet paper, I joked I would use an old T-shirt, wash it out, and wear it as a tie-dye. I would tell everyone, "Hey, at least I finally got my crap together!"

There were moments when all that mattered was saving a life, no matter the cost. I remember a young patient in critical condition, slipping into respiratory distress. I couldn't let her die—not that day, or any day. So, without thinking twice, I ran into her room without my personal protective equipment on and tried to restore her breathing. A few minutes later, Mae, a fellow nurse and good friend on the night shift, came in to help. She gently reminded me I was exposed to a COVID-positive patient. She handed me a pair of gloves and, once the crisis was over, we left the room and headed to the decontamination area for our post-crisis review.

During our discussion, Mae looked at me and said, "Did you realize you had your hands on that patient without gloves? No mask, shield, or gown. You do know she was COVID-positive, right?" To be honest, I hadn't even thought about it. I was so tired of watching people die, so focused on doing whatever it took to save another. And she was so young—far too young. I gave Mae's comment some thought, then looked at her and said, "Mae, do you realize I was homeless for over twenty-three years, eating out of dumpsters, and injecting all sorts of drugs into my body? After all that, do you really think my immune system would let COVID in?" We both smiled and got back to work. I never got COVID. God had given me a strong immune system to fight off that virus.

That same year, the book *From Park Bench to Park Avenue* was launched.

Chapter Two
CONFUSED

The Book

Since March 29, 1999, I had been sharing my truth openly and honestly, and many who listened called it miraculous. Some even called me a statistical anomaly—someone who defied all odds given where I came from. They urged me to write a book. I have always kept journals throughout my life, sharing pieces of my story at the many 12-step meetings I attended. Even when I lived on the streets, I wrote. I called the collection "Life! What About It?" But because of my countless incarcerations, those journals were lost.

Now, with more stability in my life, I chose to dedicate two years to writing my story. Putting pen to paper was no easy task, and reflecting on my past had a way of changing me. I saw patterns in my behavior. Some were worth keeping, while others I needed to leave behind. Through the writing process, I laughed, cried, got angry, but also discovered countless reasons behind my actions. I found closure, but also found new possibilities, doors waiting to be opened. I knew this was something worth sharing, to see if others found themselves in similar struggles, and maybe they could learn from them, too. I smile when I think about finishing the completed manuscript, because that's when I was hired at the college, stepping into yet another new beginning.

Once officially on staff at the college, there were still a few required classes I had to attend as part of the orientation process. During this time, I met Sherry Ward, another faculty member who led a seminar on human trafficking awareness. I had taken notes, intending to use the information later, when at the end of her presentation, she held up a book titled *My Name is Also Freedom*. She was also a publisher and had worked on this book.

When I heard this, a powerful sense struck me—I was exactly where I was meant to be, at this perfect moment. Here I was, with a completed manuscript in hand, sitting in a class led by a publisher. Was this a coincidence or divine intervention? I've always believed that nothing happens by mistake in God's world, so I approached her.

Faith requires practice, and there were too many signs to call it a coincidence. I knew, without a doubt, that God's hand was involved. I told her I had written a book and hoped to have it published. As the class cleared out—at least it felt that way in the moment—Sherry smiled and said something that convinced me I was exactly where God intended. She asked, "Is it okay if I pray with you?" Without hesitation, I replied, "Okay!" And right then, she prayed over me and my book.

I wrote that book while juggling two jobs, attending school, and in the midst of the COVID pandemic. Despite all that, *From Park Bench to Park Avenue* was published. We held the release party on April 25, 2020, via Zoom. My original plan was to print just 100 copies and give them to my friends and close associates. Little did I know, God had bigger plans in store. I never imagined what would come next. That book took on a life of its own, and through it, many eyes were opened. All I can say is that I did the footwork and left the results in God's hands.

I was excited and wanted to show-and-tell this accomplishment. So, as COVID restrictions lifted, I handed out those 100 books, starting with my friends at The Friendship Club. I thought this would be the extent of it. Just knowing that someone *knew* I was a writer was enough to make me happy. But after the book launched, videos supporting it were created, with Sherry playing a key role (this was her area of expertise). Things soon went beyond anything I had anticipated. Around this time, Nancy Clark introduced me to Jodi Barber, and we hit it off immediately. Jodi is a passionate advocate for those impacted by addiction and has produced a powerful documentary called *Overtaken*. After reading my book, Jodi connected me with Christine Devine from FOX News in Los Angeles, and Christine introduced me to Dr. Drew Pinsky, the renowned media personality and addiction medicine specialist. I just wrote the book, and God took care of the rest. Suddenly, I was doing interviews and podcasts everywhere—making headlines in newspapers, appearing on radio shows, and even recording a video with radio personality and comedian Adam Carolla. We filmed it in his studio. I have a cool photo of us sitting in his green room and another with him by his race cars. Remembering these moments still brings a smile to my face. And those memories sit right alongside the ones from when people avoided me, while I was scavenging for food in dumpsters!

Opened Eyes

Writing that book forced me to journey back to my childhood and relive some long-buried memories. I explored the abuse, addiction, homelessness, time in jail, struggles with education and employment, and many other experiences, drawing from the clearer, more positive memories I could recall. As I put these truths on paper, with eyes wide open, I soon saw my life in a new light. More than just sharing my story, I discovered a deeper hope, that others could also find the courage to be themselves, to feel safe in their own skin. In the process, I unintentionally uncovered parts of myself I didn't even know existed.

As my eyes were opened, confusion was the first to greet me. *Who am I?* I wondered. But uncertainty eventually gave way for something deeper to emerge: a chance to uncover, discover, and let go of the things that had held me back, the things that created barriers to my growth. I realized how important it is for a person to truly understand who they are and never stop searching for that truth.

So here I am, diving into yet another adventure in this thing called life, but this time, I am learning to approach it with my eyes wide open. There is so much to discover, so little time to explore it all, and so much to do before I'm done. But the million-dollar question is: *What* should I do?

During my graduate studies, I worked on developing a theoretical model designed to help homeless individuals transition off the streets. I called this model *Brown Manor*. From there, I set out to turn that concept into reality. Having spent decades on the streets and then finding my way out, I thought, why not build a "how-to" model based on my own experiences? My goal with *Brown Manor* was to provide a place of transition, a safe space where people could get the support they needed to move forward.

I planned to fund the construction of the project through sales from my first book. I knew it was an expensive undertaking and that it would require time, money, and a lot of faith. They say that progress is a process, and not to quit before the miracle happens. I believe that's true. So with this book, too, it is for the same cause: to raise money so no one has to sleep in the rain and to learn more about why we do the things we do.

Future Planning

Brown Manor is located in Mansfield, Ohio, not far from the Ohio Reformatory, a landmark known for its role in *The Shawshank Redemption*. I guess that is fitting, in a way.

The Ghetto Practitioner

This old house in northeast Ohio is in need of attention, and I am always searching for new ways to generate funding for this redemptive project, or, perhaps more importantly, inviting others to join me in the mission. I've always believed that if you aim for the stars and land on the moon, at least you've left the planet.

I've written letters to well-known figures like Oprah Winfrey, Steve Harvey, Dave Chappelle, and Tyler Perry, hoping they would lend a hand in helping get people off the streets. So far, there's been no reply. But it is what it is, and I've long since learned to just do the work and leave the results to God. I keep pushing forward, as I always have. With God by my side, that's enough for me.

My original plan was to split my time between California in the winter and Mansfield in the summer, where I could oversee the project. But as the saying goes, when I make plans, God laughs. Every time I see someone living on the streets, I feel an undeniable urgency to act. Over time, I've realized that it takes a bold and brave leader to take on such a mission. So, I hold on to the belief that, as the saying goes, "One light does make a difference."

In my third year of working at Cypress College, I pursued a master's degree in nursing. After all, I needed funds for Brown Manor, and becoming a nurse practitioner seemed like a good way to generate more income. Most of my friends from The Club looked at me like I was losing it again; I already had two full-time jobs and was about to add full-time school to the mix. On top of that, I had picked up more contracts with C.A.R.E. (Coordinating & Assisting Recovery Environments, a comprehensive mental health aftercare service). But despite how insane it might have seemed, there was something deeper driving me. I was determined to work hard—filling my schedule gave me a sense of purpose. Even my boss at Cypress College, Mr. Ramos, grew concerned and held a "mini intervention" to let me know he thought I was overdoing it.

I wasn't as young as I used to be, and I had started noticing small changes. The black Fossil wristwatch I wore felt looser, and I had to punch another hole in my belt to keep it snug. *Was I losing weight?* Maybe all the stress from being so busy was taking its toll. Then came the day Mr. Ramos called me into his office. He told me I could no longer work two full-time jobs—I had to choose one. Would I stay at Westminster TRC or continue at the college? Under no circumstances would I be allowed to work full time at both. To make matters worse, I had just failed a class because I hadn't earned the required B-minus to progress in my master's program.

Reluctantly, I stayed full-time at Cypress College and said goodbye to Westminster TRC, the company that had employed me for fifteen years and given me my first management position. Deep inside, I knew it was the right decision, even though part of me wanted to keep everything going. But I needed to focus on my master's program, and that required all of my attention.

The Ghetto Practitioner

Strange, Weird, and I Don't Know

Some might wonder if my busyness stemmed from being a workaholic. The signs were there, and it forced me to contemplate the question. Given my past as an alcoholic, I still carry some of that "alcoholic thinking." I've come to terms with that, and I'm not ashamed of it. I surrendered to that truth long ago. But as for being a workaholic, I had to take a deeper look inside to truly understand what was driving me. To gain a better understanding of who I truly am, I needed to adopt a new philosophy into my life's practice, to add another set of tools to my "toolkit for life." I eliminated certain words, phrases, and statements from my vocabulary to find the root cause of my behavior. I consciously removed words like "strange," "weird," and the phrase "I don't know," and committed to understanding the deeper reasons why these expressions no longer served me.

When you label something as "strange," it often means you haven't fully understood it yet. Take homelessness, for example. It remains an ongoing issue in today's world, but there's nothing inherently strange about it. One of the main reasons homelessness persists is because people continue to propose and implement methods that simply don't work. It's really that simple, yet we still treat it as a complex problem and struggle to find effective solutions. I strongly believe that the lack of real progress is tied to money, fear of the unknown, and those who seek to maintain absolute power. There's truly nothing strange about that.

When we think something is "weird," it often just means it's different and requires understanding. Take my relationship with a stuffed mascot named Bunny, for example. Many would probably find it strange for someone my age to have a stuffed toy, and even weirder that I talk to him sometimes! But the understanding comes when I explain that Bunny is my ultimate coping strategy and stress reliever. With all the tests and deadlines of higher education, plus the stress of working in a psychiatric facility, life can get overwhelming. But with Bunny, I can unload all my stress, and it stays between us. The serious matters in my life, all the things I need to get off my chest, I can share with Bunny, and he just smiles back at me. With him, it's completely safe to express my opinions without harming anyone, because Bunny talks only to me (though he does have other friends like Uncle Nate and Aunt Kay, but that's another story). He's also the perfect companion for political discussions!

Now, let's talk about the phrase, "I don't know." When you use it, it often feels like you're unsure or struggling to articulate what's on your mind. But deep down, you probably do know what you want to say; it's just a matter of finding the right words. By removing this phrase from my vocabulary, I've learned so much more about myself and what life has to offer. This might be a bit of a rant, but I hope it helps you.

So, back to whether I'm a workaholic—I can confidently say that I do have an addictive personality. This trait shows up in many areas of my life. Now what do you think about that?

The Ghetto Practitioner

Who Am I?

But the real question, I believe, is: Who am I? I can say with complete certainty that my life is rooted in my relationship with God. Everything I do flows from that connection. Years ago, I had a powerful spiritual awakening that changed the trajectory of my life. He responded not just with words, but with an overwhelming serenity that has guided me ever since.

So, who am I? I am someone still learning, still evolving, still showing up for life—especially when life gets lifey. Now the next question is: Where am I?

Where Am I?

When I was sleeping on the streets and in abandoned houses, deep in addiction and survival mode, my entire worldview was upside down. What was wrong looked right. What was harmful felt comforting. What was deadly seemed beneficial to me. I was living in the negative—like the negative side of a Polaroid photo, barely recognizable, not even to myself. It wasn't living. It was existing.

I had no real way to shower, no steady food to eat, no safe place to call home, no sense of self-worth or purpose—just drifting and numb. I had become disconnected from who I was, and even further from who I was meant to be.

But somewhere in that darkness, a light started flicker-
ing. I came to realize I was a lost soul—exhausted, empty, but
still breathing. That was the beginning of my discovery.

Knowing—that's what truly opened the doors to living
life right side up. It wasn't money, pleasure, or simply doing
what felt good in the moment. Don't get me wrong, money is
important, but real wealth begins in the mind. Education is
vital. Investing in my thinking and embracing education became the bridge to transformation. I still believe that the more
you know, the more you grow, and sometimes that growth requires letting go of old habits, outdated beliefs, and lingering
pain. That's how forward movement happens. Now, I have the
freedom to choose where I live, where I work, what I eat, and
how I spend my time. And that kind of freedom? It started in
the mind long before it ever showed up in my reality.

These days, I'm just a regular person who works steadi-
ly to take care of myself. I drive a car with four matching tires,
wear clean clothes—pressed most of the time—and I shower
daily and use deodorant. This is my new normal. It may seem
simple, but it's a life I once only dreamed about. Spiritually, I'm
in a safe place now, grounded by a relationship with a loving
God who is still in the miracle business. He keeps my world
from spinning out of control. God is my rock. Over time, and
often through trial and error, I've learned that prayers aren't
answered like instant mashed potatoes. Just because you're in
hot water doesn't mean you'll get instant results. Growth takes
time, and peace often arrives quietly.

The Ghetto Practitioner

Experiencing life is a lot like driving a car: you keep your eyes focused on the road ahead, glancing in the rearview mirror just enough to stay aware, but not so long that it takes your attention from where you're going. If I were to pull over, it would only be to ask myself, "Am I still headed toward the happy destiny God has planned for me?" But truth be told, there's no real need to stop at all if I let God drive and just trust in the journey. Funny how most of our problems seem to show up when we insist on taking the wheel ourselves. I guess that means that where I am, I am supposed to be!

Something's Not Right

With clarity regarding who I am and where I am supposed to be, I admit, how I got there involved some addiction to work. My full-time job at Cypress College had me teaching clinicals on Mondays and Tuesdays—ironically, at the same facility I had just left—which gave me the chance to still see old friends like Mae, Kitzy, Nancy, and Sheila. Wednesdays and Thursdays were for classroom instruction with my co-teacher, Draguna, and Fridays were dedicated to lesson planning. Everything felt steady, even peaceful. Life was finally moving smoothly—not a cloud in sight. At least, that's what I thought… until the day we took a field trip to the Museum of Psychiatry in Los Angeles. That's when I started feeling it—that subtle nudge that something wasn't quite right.

During our tour of the museum, I found myself fascinated by the long, complicated history of mental health treatment. Many of the methods used in the past were downright barbaric, yet somehow justified in the name of science. As we entered an exhibit featuring various forms of lobotomies, I became lightheaded. Whether it was from the pungent smell of formaldehyde lingering in the air or the unsettling visuals of the torturous "treatments," I couldn't say for certain. But I began to shiver as a chill ran through my body, followed by a flash of heat. Perspiration poured down my forehead and arms, and my stomach exhibited hyperactive bowel sounds—a loud, gurgling protest, sending a clear signal that something wasn't right.

Feeling weak, I sat down on a nearby bench, and everything got hazy. The next thing I remember, I was lying on the museum floor, surrounded by my students. I had blacked out. According to them, I had been unconscious for several minutes. Waking up to that scene was mortifying. Here I was, their college instructor on a professional field trip, now the center of attention for all the wrong reasons. To make matters worse, an ambulance was already in route. When the paramedics arrived, they checked my vitals. My blood pressure was low, but quickly returned to normal. While I've been diagnosed with high blood pressure (hypertensive) in the past, this was the opposite: I was *hypo*tensive. The paramedics strongly urged that I go to the hospital, but I declined. I figured, after everything I'd been through—addiction, homelessness, carnival life, working through the peak of COVID—a little dizziness didn't seem like a death sentence.

The Ghetto Practitioner

I assured them and my co-instructor, Marcos, that I'd follow up and take care of myself. That seemed to satisfy them, and the situation deescalated. Marcos even took me out for a meal to help regain my strength. Looking back, I guess that was a dramatic way to score a free lunch!

A few days later, I followed up with my doctor and described what had happened at the museum. After listening, he diagnosed me with vasovagal syncope—essentially, a fainting spell triggered by a sudden drop in heart rate and blood pressure, often caused by an overreaction to stress or stimuli. He reassured me it wasn't life-threatening and sent me on my way. But even with a medical explanation in hand, I couldn't shake the feeling that something deeper was going on. That incident had left an imprint on me. From that moment on, I became hyper-aware of my body and surroundings. Every time I stepped into the classroom, I'd either sit while teaching or stand near a chair, just in case that strange sensation came back. I wasn't about to let myself collapse in front of my students again.

Still, as much as I tried to carry on like nothing was wrong, I sensed that this was only the beginning of something much bigger unfolding beneath the surface. I just didn't want to admit it yet.

Is Denial Dangerous?

My career has given me the privilege of working with individuals across the entire spectrum of mental health, substance use, and developmental disabilities. A few years ago, my friend Mary Palafox introduced me to a board dedicated to supporting individuals living with severe mental illnesses—particularly schizophrenia. Always eager to learn and absorb new insights, I found myself intrigued by the topic. I've always embraced the idea that "more is better" with knowledge, so when Mary invited me to join the Schizophrenia and Psychosis Action Alliance as a board member, I was both excited and humbled. It was my first time serving on a board, and the experience has truly expanded my understanding of schizophrenia and the systems surrounding it.

I was trained to recognize schizophrenia as a serious and complex mental condition, one that becomes increasingly difficult to manage as a person ages. This illness has both positive and negative symptoms, and one of its most defining traits is that individuals with schizophrenia rarely realize they have it. This is because of a condition called anosognosia, where a person cannot recognize or acknowledge their own health issues. For years, I believed that people with severe mental illness were either in denial or simply poor historians of their own experiences. However, my understanding has evolved.

I began to wonder: could this phenomenon also apply to addiction?

Could people who abuse alcohol experience something similar to anosognosia? I know that prolonged alcohol abuse can lead to Korsakoff Syndrome, a form of amnesia.

The Ghetto Practitioner

When I was drinking and using drugs, I never thought I had a problem. In fact, I didn't realize just how maladjusted I was to life until that police officer asked me if I needed help one day. Looking back on it now, I wonder if I had anosognosia. But if I can recognize all of this now, perhaps it fits more into the realm of denial. Maybe this is why I ignored what had happened at the museum.

Denial is dangerous, but there's no denying that what happened that day at the museum was real. With all my years in the healthcare field, I know your body speaks to you. And that day, mine was definitely trying to grab my attention. After the incident, I began feeling more and more exhausted every day, and developed an insatiable craving for ice chips. On top of that, there was a mild, persistent pain radiating from the lower right side of my abdomen. Of course, I ignored it. I figured it would go away on its own, right? I chalked it up to the typical aches and pains of growing older and working hard. So, I just kept pushing forward, believing the old saying, "What doesn't kill you will make you stronger."

As I teetered on the edge of ignoring my body's warnings, I couldn't shake the feeling that something more was at play.

Maybe God was trying to send me a message. Was I willing to listen to what He was saying?

Chapter Three
TEETERING

Not far from the intersection of Harbor and Wilson, where my life was once at a standstill, is a park located on Hamilton Street. In California, sleeping on a park bench is much more doable in the cold winters than it is in Ohio. But here on Hamilton Street, there is a bench that holds special meaning to me. One night, years ago, I asked God to prove Himself to me there in that park. The response was indeed profound when "something" happened; a peace and calmness penetrated my soul. That is when I received my three mandates from God. It has now become a routine for years, to visit that place at night alone, to think about how my life used to be, and to pray. I feel so grateful for the life I had been given. On that specific night, I was praying and meditating, and a thought entered my mind. I closed my eyes and lifted my head toward the stars and asked God an important question.

"God, I know cars run on gas, and I know that this bench I am sitting on is solid. Prove to me You exist, and I'll do whatever You want me to do." I stayed quiet and felt a breeze touch my face. The wind blew more strongly than usual, and in that moment, I knew that something profound had just shifted inside me.

The Ghetto Practitioner

The leaves on the tree appeared larger than normal, profoundly three-dimensional and awash in bright pastel colors. An overwhelming calmness flowed through my body, surreal and peaceful. I bowed my head toward the ground and noticed that the bench was surrounded by tiny animals that had come out of the wooded area. I cried, and my life's mandate was given to me as I felt this presence say, *"You are to never hate anymore, you are to never intentionally harm anyone anymore, and you must finish everything that you start."* I cried once more, closed my eyes, and lay down on the bench. I stayed there for a while and thought about everything that had just occurred—and I still do today. It was then that I realized I had received the Holy Spirit.

The Holy Spirit

I was taught that our spiritual awakenings sometimes come in the form of education. For me, this means that certain experiences happen in the moment, and later on, we learn how to label or understand them. This was certainly the case for me. Many years later, I came to realize the profound gift God had given me that night. The way I came to accept it was rather interesting. There's a saying, "When the student is ready, the teacher will appear." It was only later that I understood what that truly meant.

The unfolding of this gift began when my friend Jodi introduced me to Cheryl Hill. Cheryl, a broadcaster with the **Holy Spirit Broadcasting Network,** hosts a show called

Generational Health and Wellness. With her bright smile and vibrant energy, Cheryl is a beacon of positivity. After a brief conversation, I gave her a copy of my book, and she found my story captivating and inspiring, and introduced me to Pastor Debbie Aimer from **Butterfly Ministries,** suggesting that my story would be a great fit for her show.

Pastor Debbie read my book, and while we were having lunch at Nordstrom's Café in Southern California, she asked if I would like to be interviewed on her show. Of course, I agreed, and before I knew it, I was sitting in a studio doing a televised recording. We discussed my book and the incredible journey God had taken me on, bringing me to where I was meant to be. After the taping, I received a call from Apostle Bills himself, asking if we could meet.

Apostle Andrew Bills is a tall African American man with a deep, warm voice that radiates love. I met him at the HSBN studios, and his smile was like a beacon of light. We sat down for about thirty minutes, and I shared my story with him. He nodded, listened intently, and with excitement. I felt so safe in his presence, as if I could confess everything I had ever done without fear of judgment.

After our conversation, he introduced me to Richard, a producer at HSBN, and his wife, Anne Marie. We recorded a 30-minute interview for Apostle Bill's show. Afterward, he invited me to host a program of my own! As I've said many times before, I wholeheartedly believe nothing in God's world happens by mistake. That day marked the beginning of *I Once Had Nowhere to Go,* and I've been doing the show ever since.

I still smile in awe and amazement at how far God has brought me in life. I can see all the puzzle pieces coming together to reveal an incredible picture! God wanted me to truly understand what to call the internal gift He had given me years ago. So, I opened my Bible once more, seeking points of reference to help guide me as I prepared for my show.

As I flipped through the pages of that small red book, memories of my time in prison resurfaced, reminding me to remain humble. Rereading the Bible, new insights and revelations, things I had missed in the past, were unveiled. It's fascinating how the same passages can reveal entirely different lessons each time you read them.

I was reminded that Jesus had died so I could receive this precious gift. I now felt armed with the truth. I also remembered that when you ask God for something, He gives it to you when you are truly ready. So, here I was, on fire with my new discovery, and grateful to have the words to explain why I was so blessed to do what I do.

Many of my friends have asked me how I've been able to accomplish so much in life, especially considering where I came from. Now I have the right answer to give them: it was because I received the Holy Spirit years ago.

But, just because you have this gift doesn't mean life will be easy!

I was in the studio filming one day when my phone went off (it was on silent, so I didn't think much of it). The show must go on, and that day, I could feel the Spirit working through me. After the filming wrapped up, I checked my phone and saw the call was from my school counselor. She was informing me that the deadline to take a crucial test had passed, and as a result, I had failed the course. I was stunned! I was just four weeks away from completing the entire program.

I immediately called her back. Apparently, the test I had missed was available from Sunday to Wednesday, but I was certain the schedule said it was *Wednesday to Sunday.* And today was Thursday! I couldn't help but wonder—since the Holy Spirit dwells within me—*shouldn't I have been blessed with some divine intervention to help keep me on track and ensure I stayed on top of everything?*

My emotions ran through the entire spectrum of Elizabeth Kubler Ross's stages of grief—first, Denial, then Anger, followed by Bargaining, Depression, and finally, Acceptance—all in the span of sixty minutes! I argued with my counselor, insisting she was wrong, and by God, I was going home to check my computer and prove it to her. I kept venting, complaining that the school was just out for money, and threatened to quit and find another college to finish the course. Oh, I really let her have it, all the while still holding on to the persona of the spiritual guru I had just professed to be only minutes earlier, speaking confidently on camera!

I was visibly upset, but practicing life is a constant balancing act—an ongoing tug-of-war between choosing faith or giving in to how I feel; between trusting and letting go, or holding on too tightly to my "right" to control things. When you accept the Holy Spirit, it doesn't mean that your thoughts, actions, and situations are instantly perfect; it simply means they are now guided by this divine presence. So, I took the necessary steps and prayed.

Once I got home, I opened my computer and, sure enough, I had misread the days. My mind raced through a plethora of options, including dropping out entirely. But then I prayed again and was reminded of my mandate to finish everything I start. I swallowed my pride, called my counselor, apologized for my attitude and behavior, and asked what the next step was. She told me I would have to repeat the class. This time, I bit my tongue and cried out to God, Who gently guided me to enroll in the next available class. *And* to put my test dates on a calendar so I didn't miss any more exams. That day, I walked away with a valuable lesson: God is still in charge, and when I make plans, He often laughs!

Now, that lesson learned would soon prepare me for something much bigger, a path toward becoming a Nurse Practitioner.

Nurse Practitioner

I was bored one day when the thought of becoming a nurse practitioner came to me. I had already completed my bachelor's in nursing, so why not go for a master's degree? And although some friends thought I was crazy (sorry, Mae), God was with me, and with the Holy Spirit guiding me, I couldn't go wrong. I went for it and committed to the two-year program of advanced nursing studies.

Most of the program was online, but halfway through, we had to record videos of our assessments and send them in for our teachers to review and approve. My friend, Jasper, graciously volunteered to be my "patient" for exams covering the gastrointestinal, respiratory, and cardiac systems, as well as the head, ears, eyes, nose, and throat. He even let me practice my neurological exam on him. His wife, Katie, stepped in to help with the musculoskeletal exam. They were hands-down the best patients a nurse practitioner student could ask for. But the patient who always keeps those days alive in my memory is Gilbert.

Gilbert was my final volunteer patient for the assessment skills lab, and the last exam was a full head-to-toe assessment—an intense, one-hour-and-twelve-minute exam. I needed an 85% to pass, and anyone who knows Gilbert understands this was no small feat! During the numerous retakes, we laughed and joked, leading to countless "do-overs." But after all the fun and frustration, we finally made it through, and I passed that portion of the program.

The Ghetto Practitioner

Gilbert is one of my sponsees, and I am proud of the work he is doing with his life. He often makes sure that everyone in the room knows the day when I did his assessment. He would start off by saying, "I am so proud of Anthony. When he was going through school, he had me naked on his bed, checking me out." Which was hilarious and a bit awkward at the same time. Now let me set the record straight here: all he had to do was remove his shirt during the examination, and I've got the video to prove it! So there, Gilbert, and yes, you are one man I am not ashamed to say I love.

One skill I truly excelled at and enjoyed was suturing. There was something satisfying about stitching up open wounds and perfecting different knots. However, learning to perform a well-woman exam...that wasn't exactly my favorite part of the training. But I did what I had to do and pushed through it.

As for men and prostate exams… well, enough said.

As the end of the program neared, and with the gift of a chance to repeat my final class, I couldn't help but thank God that the assessment portion was finally behind me. I was now in the clinical rotation phase, which felt like a breath of fresh air. But the timing was precarious—I had been in the middle of packing up my life for a move. Most of my textbooks were already in boxes, ready to be shipped off by the movers. All the research papers I'd accumulated over the years were now in the dumpster behind my condo. My once-proud home office, complete with five filled bookcases, had been disassembled. The multiple computers I had scattered across my home were boxed up or sold off—except for the one I kept on the dining table. There was no room for error. It was all or nothing. Every moment felt like a conversation with God, teetering on the edge of what I could handle.

My living space had been stripped down to the bare essentials: a sofa, a chair, and an air mattress where I slept each night. The television was gone, so was the stereo, and the kitchen was a ghost town—no pots, no pans, not even a single plate. All the food had been tossed, and my once-massive stash of COVID-paranoia days toilet paper had dwindled to one lonely roll hanging on the holder.

The only thing left between me and graduation and my move east was my capstone project, a detailed, research-backed proposal outlining how to implement a cognitive-based transitional care program. In theory, I was ready. Years earlier, I had created a rough prototype of this concept when I launched C.A.R.E., but now the stakes were higher. This version had to be built from the ground up, designed specifically for individuals experiencing homelessness, and channeled it into something that could actually change lives.

With just one week left before my departure from California, I crossed the finish line, graduating from the nurse practitioner program with a solid B-.

The Ghetto Practitioner

On December 20, 2023, I locked the door to my condo for the very last time. It was a bittersweet goodbye to the only place I had ever truly called home. That house was more than just four walls; it was the first property I had ever owned, and the first space I lived in after beginning sober living two decades earlier. Through every high and low, I held on to that place. I closed the door to that part of my life and got ready for another adventure, a new season of my life.

It was surreal to think that, years ago, I had left Ohio in search of something greater in California. And now, after forty-four years of lessons, losses, growth, and grace, I was boarding a plane back to where it all began. I wasn't running away this time. I was returning—transformed.

Ohio

Off to the East Coast I went. Even now, people ask why I chose Mansfield, Ohio, of all places. It's a question I've heard repeatedly from friends, strangers, and even from former Ohio Senator Sherrod Brown himself. But my answer never changes: I didn't choose Mansfield—God did. This journey isn't mine to script, but His, and Brown Manor is a huge part of it.

Given my distant past, finding employment wasn't easy. It took time, persistence, and more emails than I care to count, but I was eventually offered a position as a nurse at Ohio Health Hospital in Mansfield.

It had also become increasingly difficult to manage Brown Manor from California. While Brandon Minor was overseeing the project, things weren't progressing as I had envisioned. He was juggling several large projects and had generously devoted much of his spare time to developing Brown Manor for me, something I will always be grateful for. I understood that his time was limited, and I appreciated all he had done. Brandon and I had met years ago through the newspaper, and to this day, we remain close friends.

We filmed a pilot for a television show once about Brown Manor, produced by Tonier Cain, and Brandon was featured in it. He was all smiles, radiating joy throughout the production. Those times felt special, and whenever I see someone happy, I can't help but share in their joy. One day, behind the scenes, I couldn't resist and came up with a Hollywood-style nickname for him. I told him, and he smiled. From that moment on, Brandon would forever be known as Brick Mason!

Another reason I came to Mansfield was because of an attractive woman I'll refer to as "Mystery Woman" (and if she chooses to reveal herself, so be it). I met her at a fundraiser for Brown Manor, and I was immediately smitten. We were together for a brief time, and I'll admit, for a moment I thought, *maybe I won't have to worry about growing old alone anymore.* The sun seemed to shine a little brighter! But despite those high hopes, it didn't work out. Relationships have always been a tricky thing for me, and no matter who was around in my past, I often felt like I was alone inside. The presence of others never seemed to fill the void, and I've come to realize it wasn't about those around me but something deeper within. My desire for connection, paired with the drive to get Brown Manor moving, was what ultimately pushed me to Mansfield. Looking back, I see that all these experiences, even the ones that didn't last, are pieces of a bigger puzzle—a puzzle I'm still working to understand, and maybe, just maybe, it's helping me learn to stop feeling so alone.

Not in Kansas Anymore

When I finally landed in Ohio, now officially a permanent resident, my friend Doug was waiting for me at the Columbus airport. I had bought my car from him, and we drove to his place so I could drop him off. After handing me the key fob and explaining how to operate the vehicle, we said our goodbyes. As I drove away, it felt like a lifetime since I had been behind the wheel in this state. The unfamiliar roads wound through countryside that seemed alive with deer, ready to dart across my path at any moment. I couldn't help but chuckle and think, "Dorothy, you're not in Kansas anymore!"

As the miles stretched out before me, a wave of homesickness hit. I missed California—the warm sun, the sounds of the ocean, and the familiar 55 Freeway heading south, but Costa Mesa and Newport Beach weren't going to magically appear on the horizon today. Yet beneath that feeling was something stronger: faith. Faith that this was where I was meant to be. Faith that God had a purpose for me in this unfamiliar place. As I soaked in the scenery, it hit me: I was no longer the same person who left here all those years ago. No longer a drug-addicted, homeless eighteen-year-old searching for a way out, but returning as a sober-minded sixty-two-year-old with a master's degree and a purpose to make a difference. Life has been incredibly kind to me, and for that I'm grateful.

Brown Manor

The historical mansion, known as Brown Manor, is a large yellow house that sits on the corner of Sturges and First Street in Mansfield. It is a building consisting of two distinct sections, which I refer to as the old and the new. The old part was built in the early 1900s and has a Victorian feel to it. It is a three-story structure with brick walls, stained-glass windows and crystal glass throughout. It also has an attic and an attached basement. Then there's the new part, which was added in the 1950s. It has a flat roof and utilitarian design, with nothing special about it other than it provides additional bedrooms and bathrooms. Over time, within these walls, Brown Manor has been home to many ventures and people who found refuge in that space. It was once a treatment center called New Beginnings, then it became an art studio, then a thrift store. I have been told that it was once the Sturges Nursing Home, owned by Clint and Nellie Dotson back in the late 1950s and '60s, which provided services to the senior population of this area. From the view on the First Street side of the building, you can spot a room on the ground floor that was once a beauty shop called Modern Miss.

The Ghetto Practitioner

I bought Brown Manor sight unseen after a phone call with my brother, who inspired me to purchase it. Soon, it will serve as a home for others, offering them a fresh start—a future haven for those currently unhoused, and once again, a place for hope and restoration.

As I drove down State Route 13, my plan was simple: get unpacked, then head straight to Brown Manor. Each time I have stepped through the doors of this place, I am met with the stark reality that there is always more work to be done than the last time. When I called my financial managers, Maurice and Cindy, and told them of my idea to fund this project by draining my retirement funds, Maurice, whom I deeply respect and who has always had my best interests at heart, was hesitant. He didn't agree with my decision. But I persisted, and after much back-and-forth discussion, he finally relented and released my life savings. Cindy wished me luck, and I thanked them both for helping me preserve what I had saved all these years.

Even with the amount I had saved over the past twenty years, I realize now it still isn't enough to complete this massive project. But when you're driven by faith, you have more than you could ever need. It's God's money, after all, and I'm just here to manage it while I'm on this earth. None of these earthly possessions will go with me when I die. I've never spotted a hearse towing a U-Haul behind it!

There was no turning back now. I stood in the doorway of my new home and the weight of everything settled on me.

This was supposed to be a fresh start, but all I could feel was exhaustion. The trip had drained me, and the overwhelming sense of isolation was now amplified in this empty space. That night, as I lay down to sleep, the quiet of this unfamiliar place stirred my restless thoughts and I could not find peace. And just like that, a new companion introduced itself, one I hadn't expected but was now impossible to ignore.

Mister Insomnia

Mr. Insomnia does his best work at night and, of course, he wants me to be his company. It doesn't matter how tired I am, he's there, with no respect for what I have to do the next day. He's rude like that, but he always manages to grab my attention, opening my eyes to whatever he wants me to see. Tonight, he wanted to talk about Brown Manor and all the work that still needs to be done. He reminded me of how the wind had been vicious lately, tearing through one of the large broken stained-glass windows that was about to fall out. I told Mr. I. that I had spoken with Bob, and he said he would remove the pieces of glass and replace the open area with some type of covering so the rain wouldn't soak the walls again. Mr. I. said that he understood, but then mentioned the water company's complaints about a pipe that still needs to be connected. I told him Brandon was on it, but then he hit me with a sobering question: "Where are you going to get more money for all this?"

Before answering him, I had one of my own, hoping to shut him up for once. "Is this going to be a long night?" Mr. I.

laughed and told me to put the coffee pot on. I didn't find that one bit amusing and looked over at Bunny, who chuckled, too. I snapped at my blue fuzzy friend. "You need to focus on your own life," I said. That's when he quietly whispered to me, "Not if Seymour gets too big, I won't."

There was something about the randomness of this statement that reminded me of that day at the museum in L.A.—the strange, unsettling feeling I'd gotten, like things were just off and I couldn't figure out why. I sighed and took a deep breath, but as I did, a slight twinge of pain shot through my side. It wasn't a comfortable feeling. The weight of it all pressed in—this new chapter of my life, the uncertainty, and the lingering exhaustion.

It was my first day in the new house, and hanging out with Mr. Insomnia for too long makes you reflect on a lot of things. I once heard that when you're alone with only your thoughts, you're hanging out with bad company. I glanced at Bunny, puzzled by his mention of Seymour. Was Bunny secretly some kind of alien with telepathic powers, gifted with insight beyond my understanding? I smiled, holding the stuffed toy dressed in his tie-dyed hippie shirt, and looked into his black buttoned eyes. "Who is Seymour?" I asked, but Bunny didn't say a word (well, actually, I have never heard him verbally speak back to me), but I couldn't help but feel that he was holding something back.

Maybe I'm losing my mind. Maybe Mr. Insomnia is getting to me more than I realize. I tossed Bunny onto the bed, and he landed on his belly, his shirt crumpled beneath him, and without a peep.

My thoughts teetered all night, swinging between clarity and chaos. I kept thinking about the way I've had to tighten my belt—*am I losing weight?* Then my mind flashed to that humiliating moment when I passed out during the field trip... a memory I'd rather forget, but one that keeps showing up uninvited.

For most of my early life, I abused a lot of drugs, particularly stimulants. It's why I am forced to entertain guests such as Mr. Insomnia (or is it just the swirl of everything happening all at once, making it hard to see the light at the end of the tunnel?) Over the years, I have learned to capitalize on this odd nighttime friendship. Typically, I get up and work on something in the house or lie there thinking about life.

I think about all those years I wandered aimlessly throughout life. I do believe I have learned my lesson. I never want to alter my mind or mood with chemicals and experience the high cost of low living again. Addiction is a terrible thing to go through. Today, fentanyl is taking lives at a devastating pace, leaving families shattered and communities hollowed out.

So many lives are affected—this is why Brown Manor will be a drug-free environment with the philosophy to make an effective change within oneself, keeping the mind clear.

The Ghetto Practitioner

I know from experience that it is hard to retain information if your brain is saturated with drugs and alcohol. The obvious solution to drug addiction is complete abstinence, of course.

I know from personal experience how hard it is to hold on to anything meaningful when your brain is fogged with substances. That's why the foundation of this place has to be built on sobriety, growth, and the quiet strength of clarity. For those willing to do the work, it's more than possible—it's transformative.

Thoughts like these race through my mind, and tonight, I can't seem to shut them off, and the only one I have to share them with is Bunny. Finally, exhaustion overtakes me. I pick Bunny up and gently place him on the table next to the bed. I close my eyes and exhale deeply, grateful that Mr. Insomnia is done with me—at least for tonight.

Chapter 4
WANDERING

Upon Awakening

Two weeks had passed since that first restless night in my new home. I had settled into a rhythm—well, sort of. Each morning, I hit my knees before I hit my feet, reciting the Third Step Prayer, something I have done for years. It anchors me, a reminder of the path I'm on. Today, I also sat by the side of my bed and felt His presence and quieted my thoughts, attentive to what He wants me to accomplish on this day.

Brown Manor renovations continued in a never-ending list of tasks demanding attention; however, Bob had removed the stained-glass window, and I hoped Vidonish Stained Glass Studios would bring it back to life. The water situation was in the capable hands of Ken, a man who preferred to stay anonymous. I wished I could give him the credit he deserved, but for now, he remained behind the scenes, working silently in the background. As I focused on these projects, the feeling of a clearer purpose emerged.

I stood in front of the mirror, putting on my navy-blue hospital scrubs for work. The routine felt grounding, and I was thankful for that. I glanced over at Alexa, the Amazon device that had become my strange new friend. For me, this device is complicated and doesn't respond well (or at all) when you call it by different names, such as Lexie. I figured that since she was in my bedroom, why not get to know each other on a personal level? "Lexie, play some Pink Floyd," I said, but she asked if I wanted to spend more money for Amazon Prime to have exclusive access to that band. I told her no, so she played Gordon Lightfoot instead.

After losing that battle, I grabbed Bunny and headed downstairs. I filled the coffee machine with water, gave a drink to my banana plant, Mussella (I call her Muse for short), and waited for the coffee maker to do its magic. As the Keurig poured its Folgers goodness into my favorite Winnie the Pooh coffee cup, I smiled and thought of that jingle from the old commercial: "the best part of waking up is Folgers in your cup." Then I took my first sip of the bitter brew, sat back on the gray sofa, and turned on the morning news.

As I watched the colorful images flash across the screen, I remembered the tiny, nine-inch black-and-white TV I'd managed to get in prison and how much it meant to me back then. Now, I had a whole house of appliances—everything I needed.

I am still learning the things some people take for granted—those spiritual, mental, emotional, and physical arenas. I have also discovered new things like crockpots, blenders, toasters, and a host of other electrical appliances. These things may seem normal to some, but I never had them when I was homeless, so they took some time for me to master. I am proud of myself and happy to share that I am now well-versed in using a blender. I can prepare (correctly) delicious blended drinks from recipes I find on YouTube. Congratulating myself, I now go by the name of Capt. Smoothie!

As the coffee slowly does its thing within my nervous system and the neurotransmitters in my brain make their way across the synapses, I decide I've had enough of the entertainment and turn off the television. I muse over the fact that, twenty-five years ago, I was in jail. It seems like a lifetime ago, and so much has changed since then. Another sip and I feel my pulse increase from the caffeinated elixir. My brain tells me I have fully awakened, so I better get ready for work. Is this what they mean by being *woke?*

Over the years, I've worn many hats, wandered down countless paths, but the one constant that's grounded me is my work in mental health. It's been two decades now, and somehow, it still feels like home. There's something sacred about walking beside those who are navigating the rough terrain of their own minds—people often labeled as "too far gone" or "difficult." I've learned that what the world calls delusion, I recognize as pain trying to make itself heard. Some folks joke it takes a special person, mildly insane themselves, to deal with complicated issues such as mental health. Maybe they're right. I wonder if this type of thinking would fall under the category of controlled lunacy?

The Ghetto Practitioner

As I head upstairs, I ask Lexie to play Eminem. Instead, she plays the Eagles. All I can do is smile, as she seems to have a mind of her own. Is this what living with artificial intelligence will be like? I sit on my bed and listen to the tunes, giving myself the gift of a minute more to think about my day at work.

Bunny is now sitting quietly on the dresser and, hopefully, safely out of trouble. Clipping on my name badge and pinning my Voicera to my scrub top, I look in the mirror and give myself one last nod of approval. No cape, no armor—just a man in navy-blue scrubs with a calling. I step out into the world with purpose.

New Job

I work the night shift just two days a week, from 7 p.m. to 7 a.m., and while most people might find those hours a bit unnatural, they suit me just fine. Mr. Insomnia would probably say I was born for it. The schedule gives me plenty of time during the week to focus on Brown Manor, and the extra income helps cover some of the ongoing costs. The unit I'm assigned to now is smaller than the ones I worked on back in the days of Westminster TRC and Fairview. Here at Ohio Health Behavioral, things are a bit more contained—three units in total: two for adults and one dedicated to the children.
I believe that nursing is a noble profession. Anyone who has invested blood, sweat, and tears to become a nurse knows that it takes a certain type of character to earn this title. The long hours, the sacrifice, and the emotional weight—it truly

takes heart, requiring more than intelligence or skill. Back in school, we used to say, "nurses eat their young," and as harsh as that sounds, there's some truth in it. Nursing school felt a lot like bootcamp. Four days a week of lectures, endless homework, study groups that stretched late into the night—and let's not forget those long clinical hours that tested not just your knowledge, but your endurance and compassion.

Still, something kept me going. Maybe it was in the quiet belief that I was meant for this. Once I finished and had that snazzy pin stuck on my chest, I felt a small sense of accomplishment. This was short-lived because then preparation was needed to pass the state boards. And once that passing score arrived, I received my license. Congratulations, now stand on your feet for twelve hours and get seasoned!

I was introduced to the world of nursing long before I ever stepped into a classroom. The first nurse I ever knew was my mother, Jeanette. She'd come home after long shifts dressed in her crisp white uniform and polished white shoes— the kind they all wore back then. I can still picture the small white cap perched neatly on her head, marked with two black stripes. I didn't understand their meaning as a child, but I later learned they signified her bachelor's degree in nursing. That silent symbol of achievement spoke volumes about the kind of woman she was—disciplined, determined, and deeply devoted to her calling.

The Ghetto Practitioner

They used glass bottles in those days, and I remember her once explaining the technique of giving an enema with a phrase I'll never forget: "high, hot, and a hell of a lot." Way to go, Mom! That was Jeanette: blunt and practical and dedicated. Now, as I walk in similar shoes, I carry her memory with me. Not just in her words or her uniform, but in the quiet strength it takes to show up, day after day, and offer healing in a world that often feels broken.

Acute Care

In the acute unit in behavioral health (where I spend most of my time these days), the doors always remain locked. It seems to have come full circle—and quite poetically—that most of my life was spent behind some type of locked door. The biggest difference is that these days I have the liberty to come and go as I please. Today, I'm using my key card to enter the outside door, then wait for that one to be secured before opening the next door into the unit. I walk through these doors not because I have to, but because I've chosen to. That freedom, that purpose, is something I never take for granted. This being my first time working at this hospital, I suppose you could say I'm still the new guy. When I was assigned to Unit C, I felt a wave of apprehension. It had been a while since I'd done hands-on care on a hospital floor, and part of me questioned if I still had the rhythm for it. But beneath all that, I was deeply grateful—grateful to have found a job so quickly here in Ohio and to be doing work that still speaks to my heart. As I stepped onto the unit that first day, I whispered a thank you to God under my breath. And before long, something familiar returned—muscle memory, maybe, or just the peace that comes from being where you're supposed to be. I found my pace walking down that long gray hallway, passing room after room until I reached the nurse's station. It felt like coming home.

There are five of us working the unit tonight: Emily, Katie, Melody, Kaitlin, and me.

Emily is the quiet type. She is gentle, kind, always offering a warm smile. She was the first to welcome me when I arrived, and her kindness immediately set the tone for my experience here. Knowing I was new to the area, she gave me a crash course in the local culture—especially the Amish community. Thanks to her, I've developed a full-blown addiction to Amish noodles and those little pies that should be illegal. They're so good.

Then there's Katie. At first glance, she seemed reserved, keeping her opinions to herself. That lasted all of five minutes. Katie doesn't mince words; she's direct, refreshingly blunt, and honest to the bone. That kind of truthfulness can rattle some people, but for me, it was comforting. I was raised around straight talk, and her candor quickly made her one of my favorite people here.

Melody is the more nurturing one of the group. She's got that motherly energy that puts everyone at ease. Always smiling, always helpful, and full of clever wit that sneaks up on you. Her sharp wit and controlled sarcasm remind me of a good spicy meal: delightful, goes down easy, and before you know it, your ass has been lit up.

And then there's Kaitlin, our PSA, who brings a thoughtful and questioning energy to the room. She's been wondering if she should go back to school, sorting through that big decision like so many of us have done at some point. It's honest, and it's real—and that vulnerability is something I deeply respect.

There are other angels also here in behavioral health who welcomed me and helped me when I had questions about how to resolve a particular situation or needed to find some paperwork. I'm surrounded by all these lovely angels on the night shift.

As time does what time does, nights turn into days and days become weeks. I pretty much followed the same routine, and things became familiar and repetitive. Before long, I was fully trained on the other units as well, including Unit A, the adolescent floor—a space with its own unique energy and delicate balance.

I've worked with juveniles before, though mostly within the realm of developmental disabilities. The youth at Fairview were often more outwardly aggressive, their behaviors loud and demanding. Here at Ohio Health, the focus leans more toward mental health, and for those of us in the field, we understand just how different the approaches in treatment must be. Working with adolescents requires a certain level of creativity and patience. I've learned that one of the most effective ways to reach them is through engagement—keeping their minds occupied with something meaningful. Puzzles, for example, have become a simple yet powerful tool. They not only help pass the time, but studies have shown they're beneficial for improving memory and cognitive function. When you are young and struggling to make sense of the world with limited tools, even a small piece of progress—like finding one corner of a puzzle fitting into place—can feel like a win.

After working one night with the kids, I went home and did some thinking. Sitting alone, a memory emerged of when my sisters and I were placed in a children's home. I must have been around eleven years old. I can't quite recall if we were put in foster care or adopted out, as the full memory escapes me now. What lingers, however, are the feelings and the sense of abandonment somewhere deep inside of me. Dave, once a counselor of mine, told me that adults cannot be abandoned. Still, there are times I feel left to navigate this world on my own. His words, though meant to be comforting, now only serve as a reminder of the void he left behind when he passed away. The world seems quieter without him, and I miss him more than I ever expected.

For some reason, God has me working at this place at this exact moment in time. Is it because I am meant to always have a job, no matter the circumstances? Or is it a reminder to remain fully self-supportive, rejecting any outside help? What is He trying to tell me? One thing that I can say for certain is that He brought me through school and placed me here at this exact moment for something. After all, everything happens for a reason, right?

In all this, I still find that God's ways are puzzling, to say the least. In the beginning of my relationship with Him, things seemed confused and random, yet somehow orchestrated. Did I have to become a drug addict and homeless just to end up being a nurse practitioner, developing a program for those still living on the streets? As with the proverbial puzzle, each adventure is its own separate piece, and eventually, we get to see the whole picture. It just takes time and, of course, practice.

Chapter Five
SEARCHING

At age twelve, I would often have these recurring dreams where I was flying—soaring high like a bird, all over the place. Or I'd be running through hidden passageways inside a big house, a place where over twenty people lived, and somehow, we were all connected. Now, I can't help but wonder: could this have been Brown Manor?

In those days, I kept a notebook by my bed to capture those elusive thoughts and dreams that seemed to carry messages I couldn't fully grasp. Some may argue that seeking to understand dreams is taboo, or goes against certain religious principles, but God gives us dreams for a reason. For me, it's not so complicated. It is easier just to do life on its terms and enjoy the ride as I cruise through this temporary place called existence, even when passing through the darkest of places.

My good friend Mommy Pat once told me that a time would come when I'd have to open "The Closet" (which meant digging into my past to see what truths might be hiding there that were affecting my present). Were all those recurring dreams alluding to the eventual day I would be here in Mansfield, Ohio, working at a mansion for homeless people, then traveling the world to promote this new concept in recovery? Hmm… is that odd or is that God?

Maybe it's not odd at all, but simply God, weaving a story I'm only beginning to uncover.

Comfort

One chilly morning, I opened my eyes to find the cozy warmth of my king-sized comforter wrapped snugly around me. Ohio's winter had settled in, and the cold seemed sharper than anything I remembered back in California. I tucked the blankie closer around my neck and chuckled softly to myself—maybe I was just getting older, or maybe I was finally feeling the weight of the seasons here.

This chilly morning gave me a perfect reason to not get up. I smiled and wondered if other people have had one of those days when you just want to stay in bed and enjoy the cozy warmth?

Hmm… Maybe that's why this thing that feels so good around me is called a comforter.

And so, I figured it was a perfectly good day to just stay bundled up like a human burrito. Stretching one arm out from the comforter cocoon, I fumbled for the remote on the bedside table and clicked on the TV. The screen lit up, giving me a quick glimpse of the world outside my fluffy fortress—same circus, different clowns. After flipping through a parade of chaos and infomercials, I finally landed on something that made sense: an episode of *Young Sheldon*. Sometimes you just need a smart kid and a laugh before facing another grown-up day.

I stared aimlessly at the screen, watching Meemaw give young Sheldon a ride to college. It felt good, and I closed my eyes. As the voices from the television slowly faded into something unintelligible, my unconscious thoughts rose to my consciousness.

I was lost once, in a hopeless state of mind and body: no place to live, no employment, no education, and absolutely no hope. I remember feeling a gaping hole in my soul, a void so black and deep that death would have been a welcome relief. I have learned to add light to that dark place, always seeking to keep that door open—wide enough for the sunlight of the Spirit to enter. The more I reveal, the better I heal. I guess there is some truth when they say that confession is good for the soul. Subconsciously, I rubbed my hand across the top of the comforter and smiled. *Things are different now,* I thought, then I whispered to God, "Thank You for all You have given me."

History Solves the Mystery

All good things must come to an end, and with a small sigh, I clicked off the television. Rolling out of bed, I dropped to my knees for my usual morning chit-chat with God. As always, I asked Him to help remove from me the bondage of self, so that I could better follow whatever His will might be for me today. I asked for the strength, courage, and the power to carry out whatever tasks He had lined up, even the ones that weren't so thrilling.

And, of course, I let Him know just how grateful I was—for the big things, like air and eyesight, and for the little luxuries, like my comforter and the batteries in the remote that allowed me to enjoy *Young Sheldon* from my cozy bed.

Then it was downstairs to fire up the trusty Keurig. As the aroma of brewing coffee filled the air, I caught sight of a suspicious ball of blue fur nearby. I poured some Folgers into my mug and shot Bunny a look. He sat there looking all innocent, which meant he was guilty of something. I wouldn't be surprised if Aunt Kay had sent him on another wild goose chase in the night, probably in search of more Amish fry pies.

Taking a satisfying sip of my coffee, I wandered into the living room and asked Lexie to play the Eagles. Instead, "Rocky Mountain High" by John Denver came floating through the speakers.

Settling into my favorite spot at the table, coffee cup in hand, I gazed out the window and found myself drifting back to thoughts of the people I had written about in my first book. Their faces and their stories, all woven into my own.

What can I do for those still out there on the streets?

It's a question that stirs in my spirit every morning. I know what it's like to be lost, overlooked, and barely holding on to hope. God didn't bring me through the fire just to sit in comfort. He saved me so I could reach back and help someone else.

Gratitude is more than a feeling; it's a call to action. And today, just like every day, I quietly ask Him for the courage to answer that call.

Taking another satisfying sip, my thoughts wander on. The homeless are everywhere: in parks, behind dumpsters, even under bridges. Here in Ohio, some seek shelter in tunnels beneath the city. No matter where they find themselves, they are exposed to the harshness of nature—the relentless cold, the scorching heat, the endless rain. It takes a toll on the body, mind, and soul.

I am committed to engaging with as many souls as I can. I listen to the language of their hearts. So many have experienced social isolation! The quiet sting of resentment that follows after overstaying their welcome with friends or relatives, only to find themselves back on the streets again. Many who were once close to their families burn those bridges, eventually causing everything to fall apart. Then there are our brothers and sisters—released from jail, unable to find a fresh start, and without any other options—who return to homelessness, caught in a cruel cycle with nowhere to go, left to return to the only reality they know: the streets.

Each story I hear is a reminder of why I can't turn away. I shake my head, pushing the weight of those thoughts aside as I savor the last sip from Winnie. I set the cup down and take a moment, feeling the warmth settle in my chest. My mind continues to churn with these reflections as I make my way to the bathroom. The cool air greets me as I step inside, the steam from the shower fogging the mirror. As the water runs, I think back to when I was emotionally illiterate, much like the other addicts I've known, unable to recognize the feelings that ran through me.

Why didn't I feel much when I had so little to feel about?

When I didn't have much, nothing to give, I really didn't feel a loss. As the hot water pours over me, I empathize when the homeless say, "A person can leave me, and after a while, I don't even notice they are gone."

Is this why I have no serious emotional connection to anyone or anything?

I guess *history* solves that *mystery*. With my eyes closed, the water washes my thoughts back to the days when I lived on a park bench and all that came with it. And for a moment, I contemplate my history and how all of this somehow ties into who I am and the struggles I still face.

History doesn't just solve mysteries—it reveals patterns, cracks in the foundation. I know the battle I'm facing isn't just about surviving. It's about learning to feel again, to connect, to understand the damage addiction has done to my heart and soul.

Addiction

The mind is a terrible thing to waste, and it doesn't function well when it's wasted, either. I've lived on both ends of that spectrum. With a certificate in addiction counseling and years spent developing programs that specialize in co-occurring disorders, I've had a front-row seat to the devastation addiction can bring. I've treated, detoxed, and walked alongside countless individuals fighting this battle. I know all too well what's at stake when this illness is left unchecked and how it can consume not just the individual, but everyone around them.

Addiction is an obsessive and compulsive need that drives harmful behaviors. If left unaddressed, it can lead to economic ruin, social isolation, and worsening health issues. Once someone falls into addiction, it creates a physiological need, a compulsion to keep using substances despite the consequences. And addiction isn't limited to drugs or alcohol—it can take many forms. Addiction can be embarrassing, even awkward, as we've all seen in the way some people act out in public, losing control and making a fool of themselves. The shame and humiliation they experience can be just as destructive as the addiction itself.

I recall an acquaintance of mine who had stopped calling me for several weeks. Then, out of nowhere, she called one morning and asked if I could come pick her up. Even though I was dealing with physical issues of my own, I wanted to be there for her. When I arrived, I could clearly see she was high on crack cocaine. Her body jerked uncontrollably, and she couldn't seem to focus on anything. I knew she was in the depths of her addiction. She needed help, and I truly believed she knew it. I wanted to help her, but things quickly unraveled. When I refused to give her money, she walked off, and what followed was a harsh, racially demeaning text that cut deeper than I expected. The whole situation was a bitter reminder of how addiction distorts everything and strips away relationships, leaving only pain and confusion behind.

I came to help a friend, but the addiction inside her wouldn't allow it.

Addiction has a way of turning a person into someone unrecognizable—from the nice, rational Dr. Jekyll to the uncaring, destructive Mr. Hyde. It's painful watching the person you know, beneath it all, struggling to break free. However, I have learned to take things like this in stride because it is not the person who is angry and out of control; *it is the addiction making her behave this way.* I am sure others have experienced this, and sometimes the only thing you can do is pray they will one day find a solution. The hardest part? Watching them stay trapped in their own mind, a prisoner to their "stinking thinking."

My question to you is this: What do you do if someone with an addiction crosses your path? Do you turn away, or do you try to help?

Stinking Thinking

Getting sober and staying in recovery is a lifelong journey. There's no magic cure, no one-time fix. It goes far beyond being merely physical. It's the psychological and emotional aspects that truly anchor the problem. It's about the thinking—the deep-rooted mindsets and thought patterns that swirl in your brain before, during, and after the behaviors. It's these thoughts, these "stinking thinking" moments, that can lead you back into the same old cycles if you're not vigilant. Understanding this is a crucial part of healing, because without addressing the mindset, recovery will always remain an uphill battle.

Dr. Drew and I have talked about this phenomenon many times. The power of thought can be just as dangerous as addiction itself. When your mind spins into obsessive thinking, it leads to impulsive behaviors that make no sense. Fortunately, after years of practicing recovery, I've learned to recognize the chaos when it starts. When my mind starts to go off the rails, I think of it as either a football game or a circus inside my head. This little trick helps me identify negative thoughts before they get out of control, sabotaging the life I've worked so hard to build. The road to our Happy Destiny isn't always as smooth as we hope. Even if things look golden on the surface, I've learned the hard way that not everything that glitters is actually gold.

The Ghetto Practitioner

My thoughts continue to flow with the hot water, and it feels amazing. I smile at the sheer luxury of it all. No one else in here with me, no time limit ticking away. It's just me, the water, and my thoughts. It's like a mini-vacation every morning. And the best part? I can use as much Dove soap as I want without being paranoid of dropping it!

How grateful I am for this little slice of freedom.

Freedom from Self

As I lather up the bar of Dove, its clean scent invigorates me, and I am struck by the realization of how often we become prisoners of our own making, locked inside a mental fortress, never realizing we hold the key.

From a young age, I built walls to protect myself from the inevitable pain of the world. They seemed like a shield, a necessary defense against hurt. Those walls remained for so long until the next thing I knew, I was a prisoner behind them—incarcerated within the fortress I had constructed. In a physical prison, there's someone on the other side who can open the door for you. But when you build your own mental and emotional walls, you come to the painful truth that no one else can open it. No one can set you free except yourself. That realization came when I finally understood that the only thing standing between me and freedom was the simple act of turning the knob.

It took years—so many years—of struggle, pain, and self-deception before I finally found the courage to let myself out. But once I did, I learned that staying free requires a conscious effort. Now, every day, I fight to stay out of that cage I created. The key is no longer hidden away; it's in my hands, and I refuse to lock myself in again.

Stepping out of the shower, I see myself in the mirror. *Have I lost weight?* I'm not sure, but the reflection makes me pause. After drying off and getting dressed, I say a quick prayer, hoping it settles my mind. Still, there's a nagging unease lingering beneath the surface, like something is off, though I can't put my finger on it. To calm myself, I open my Bible and read, hoping the familiar words soothe any hidden emotional pain conjured up by all my contemplation.

I pick up my trusted friend, that same Bible I found in the trashcan back in the late '90s. It's funny how something discarded can become so precious. Over time, I've come to rely on my connection with God, knowing He answers when I seek Him. Today, He leads me to a passage—Philippians 4:6: "Do not be anxious about anything, but in every situation, by prayer and petition, with thanksgiving, present your requests to God." I pause and meditate on those words, letting them sink in. With a sense of peace, I finish getting dressed and step out the door, ready to face whatever the day brings.

There Are Places

Whenever I find the time, I visit places that help keep my mind grounded. One of them is The Club, and the other is church. Ironically, the clubs I frequent these days aren't for drinking, but for *not* drinking. The churches I attend aren't about seeking God, but about learning how to strengthen my relationship with Him. When I go to these churches, I often find myself in the basement, sipping coffee and reflecting. There's something about that quiet space that helps me focus, away from the noise and distractions of the world above.

This is where I met Doc, Shelia, Butch, and Chuck—regulars who always seem to be there, smiling and happy to see me. There's a certain sense of belonging I feel in their presence. We talk about God and how different life is now that we've found this newfound relationship with Him. We share about our day, how far we've come, and the simple joy of being in the moment. The vibe they create is one of happiness, joy, and freedom. Shelia often brings baked goodies, and I can't resist her blueberry cake—it's absolutely delicious, as are all of her treats. It's exactly what I needed today: warm conversation, a sense of camaraderie, and friendship.

Afterward, I head to Brown Manor to check on the progress. They say progress is a process, and that couldn't be more true here. Brick Mason had hired a crew from Taylor Contracting, and with them came Beau, a familiar face. They were working on refurbishing what would soon be the dining room. I could picture future residents sitting around the table, discussing life while enjoying breakfast. The thought makes me smile as I move through the rooms. To an outsider, it might seem like chaos, but that's the nature of construction—it's messy before it becomes something beautiful.

I had planned for a quick walk-through, but I find myself sitting on the dusty main staircase, bowing my head in prayer, then just thinking.

Brown Manor is the biggest task God has assigned me so far, and if I'm being honest, it's overwhelming. Back in California, I felt connected, like I had a purpose among people who understood me. But here, in this new place, it feels so different. I barely know anyone, and I'm tackling something I only partially understand.

On paper, everything seems like it should work: the numbers make sense, the concept is solid. I've created a model like this before, but then everything was already set in place: housing, staff, funding. Now, it's all on me. And I'm not sure I'm ready for all this alone.

I shake my head slowly and whisper, "Why me, God?"

As I gaze up at the high ceilings and the stained-glass windows scattered throughout the house, tears meet my eyes. Despite the overwhelming emotions, a small smile tugs at my lips. Not too long ago, I was like this abandoned house—broken, forgotten, and in need of restoration. But just as God has worked wonders in me, I know I'm not finished yet. There's still more to be done.

God gives us a dream, but it's up to us to decide what to do with it. Along the way, I've learned that faith often comes with delays. This has been true since the days of the Bible. Nothing in this world happens instantly; challenges slow our progress, and we might face a few dead ends. Yet, through it all, one thing remains certain—God always comes through in the end.

Despite how blessed I've been, there are times I can't help but feel cursed. This previously abandoned 9,000 square-foot property has continued to challenge me at every turn. I remember the first time I stepped foot into this house, a dried-up bat clung to a light bulb by the side entrance, and the entire place reeked of mildew. The walls and ceilings were soaked with water, crumbling apart; the roof leaked in multiple spots, and the basement had suffered severe water damage. In the attic, I found several dead birds, and in the basement, a dead possum lay slowly decomposing. The windows were shattered and boarded up, and there was no water or electricity to speak of. It was a place of complete neglect.

Today, the roof has been repaired, and there are no longer any dead animals waiting to be discovered. The water-damaged walls and ceilings have been torn out. Now, sheets of drywall—donated by the two brothers from Richland Lumber—are stacked high, waiting to replace them. The electricity is up and running, and new wall sockets have been installed. A wave of gratitude sweeps over me as I take in a deep breath and whisper, "Thank You, God."

I smile as I lock the outer door and walk away. As I head to my car, I think, *one day this house will provide a sanctuary for others.* I feel empowered once more. With just enough time to make it home for a short nap before my night shift, I glance back at the building one last time, smile, and let out a contented sigh.

Chapter Six
YIELDING

Dressed in my usual blue scrubs after my morning routine, I said goodbye to my roommate and headed out the door. Oh, did I mention my roommate? She's a quiet presence around here, and our paths rarely cross. Her door is always closed, and our relationship is much like that: separate, solitary, and seldom open for conversation. But that's okay; we all need to do what we do to keep life groovy.

I arrived at work with plans to deal with the usual unusual things. There's always something unpredictable brewing here; it's what I need to keep my mind stimulated, ready to do God's will and be of service.

My work routine stays the same: I do my rounds, take care of the patients, then return to the nurses' station. But this time, as I sat at the counter doing some charting, I began to feel faint. I remember thinking *I felt this way before—that day at the museum.* My skin felt hot, and I started perspiring profusely. The hyperactivity of my bowels began as before, and suddenly, I thought I was going to pass out. I lowered my head onto the desk, trying to steady myself, but everything felt like it was slipping. Jamie noticed immediately and asked, "Are you okay?"

My response came out slurred. Without a second's hesitation, she reached into her backpack and pulled out a small, pink cylindrical object with a round head—about five inches long. She moved toward me, her eyes focused. I could barely process what was going on. Drenched in sweat, I heard the click of a switch, followed by the whirr of something mechanical. For a split second, I thought I was imagining things, but then cool air hit me—her portable fan, its blades spinning to provide relief. She took my blood pressure, and the reading was dangerously low. The rest of the staff had now gathered around me, concerned. "You need to go downstairs to the emergency room," one of them said. I didn't have the strength to argue. My body felt like it was shutting down, and I grew more disoriented with every passing second. I vaguely remember Jarrod, the safety officer, putting me in a wheelchair, and being rushed off the unit. I don't know if I was hallucinating, but I thought I heard him making siren sounds as he whisked me through the hallways down to ER.

The ER staff ran their tests and discovered I was anemic, which explained the low blood pressure. My blood levels had always been borderline, but this felt different. The doctor suggested I stay overnight for observation, but I said a firm, "no." I mean, come on, I've survived way worse than this, so why would I let something as simple as not having enough blood take me down?

They gave me a liter of fluids, and I was back on my feet, heading straight back to work. Four hours later, I wrapped up my shift with a promise to see a doctor to figure out where the bleeding was coming from.

The next day, I called my previous doctor, Dr. Davari from Kaiser, to fill him in on what had happened the night before. After hearing the details, he advised me to discontinue one of my medications and to monitor my condition closely, keeping him updated on how things progressed. Once that was settled, I reached out to Dr. Drew to share the news. Dr. Drew has always been a steady presence in my life. He is down-to-earth, a great listener, and never hesitates to take my call. When I'm unsure about something personal, he's the one I turn to. We've been friends ever since we first connected back in 2020 through an email that I'll never forget:

Anthony,

Christine Devine gave me your contact info. I work with her at Fox 11, cohosting their 7:00 show. I saw the interview she did with you and your story just stayed with me. I'm an Internist and ran several departments at a free-standing Psychiatric Hospital for over 25 years. Seeing the population I served for so many years now deteriorating on the streets drives me to distraction.

It's clear to me how we should be managing the issue, and I suspect we would share the same outlook. Given your personal experience and professional expertise, I believe you could be very effective in shaping opinion about homelessness.

I wonder if we might get on the phone together to share ideas?

Drew Pinsky MD

When I first read the email, I had to read it over several times. Then I pranced up and down my living room floor (doing my exaggerated dance moves, of course), carrying on like there was no tomorrow. I was on cloud nine; this celebrity wants to talk to me! I really didn't know how to act. I told my friend Debbie, and all she said was, "Answer him back."

Great advice. So I did.

Hello Dr. Drew,

I am honored that you would like to hear my opinions on resolving the homeless issues. It is sad that we cannot find some solution with all the resources that are out there. I do have a way that worked for me and would love to share my thoughts with you.

I do work as you know at a Psychiatric Facility, so if you called I may not be at my phone. You could always give me a number and time, and I would be more than happy to schedule our call.

*Thank you again for reaching out to me. I am truly grate-
ful to have an opportunity to share our views.*

*Kind Regards
Anthony Brown*

Shortly after that, I went on his podcast, and we've been
friends ever since. We've had countless discussions about various topics, and whenever he meets someone who could help
further my cause, he connects us.

I have often asked his advice. During COVID, he recommended a vitamin combination that kept me virus-free.
He always says, "I am always with Team Anthony," and it's one
thing that reminds me I'm never really alone in this.

I explained my anemia to him, and he suggested I take
iron supplements.

*Oh, that's right; iron helps transport oxygen through
the body!*

I thanked him and began the search for a local healthcare provider. I was grateful that God had provided me with a
job that offered health benefits. Somehow, I have two different
insurance plans—one from my employer and the other is benefits from my retirement package. What's tragic is that some of
our brothers and sisters on the streets don't have any. I wish
we had some type of law that would allow me to share mine

with them. Currently, that's not permitted, so the next obvious solution would be for me to pass the state board exam, get certified, then provide the services for free. I need to ask God about this for sure.

Acceptance

One month later, on May 23, 2024, I met with my new primary care physician. She confirmed I was indeed still anemic, and my blood levels were continuing to drop. She recommended several tests to pinpoint the source of the internal bleeding, including a CT scan of my lungs and an ultrasound of my abdominal aorta. I did the CT scan first. The results came back with one of those classic good news/bad news/ more bad news scenarios. The good news: the bleeding wasn't coming from my aorta. The bad news: they still couldn't figure out where it was coming from. The more bad news: they found "something" in my lungs—something they referred to as nodules.

I've been a smoker since I was twelve, and I kept up the habit until I was fifty-nine. Years of smoking a variety of things probably contributed to the nodules. To be honest, I never thought I'd live this long. Looking back, I truly believed I wouldn't make it past sixteen. Once I crossed that threshold, I thought, *I'll never make it to twenty-one.* But I did. And by thirty-seven, I was living sober. Now, at sixty-two, I'm still here. I figure I've got at least another fourteen years to go, maybe more. I'm aiming to hit the average male life expectancy of seventy-six, but I'm grateful just to be standing here today. Death has always managed to keep its distance. But today? I don't know...maybe today's the day it catches up with me.

Today, they discovered a 0.8 x 0.9 x 1.5 cm irregular, non-calcified nodule in my right upper lobe, along with a 0.6 cm pleural-based nodule in my right lower lobe. Life has a strange way of reminding you that you're only human. And yet, here I am, having tapped into a source that pulled me from the brink of insanity into a new life, one filled with freedom, peace, and happiness. Now, this news is threatening to yank that rug right out from under me.

All sorts of ridiculous thoughts started crashing into my brain like a freight train. I grabbed my phone and dialed Dr. Drew's number (thank God he's on speed dial now), and blurted out in a panic, "I'm going to DIE by suffocation!" Then, as if on cue, I dramatically declared I was changing my will. Forget about leaving anything to anyone—I was going to buy a U-Haul, stuff it with all my worldly possessions, and be buried with it, embalmed in the driver's seat with my hands tightly clutched around the steering wheel. I'd go down in history as the most bizarre burial in all of humanity. He, of course, stayed cool as a cucumber and told me to calm down, saying it was probably nothing to worry about. He reminded me that I had the mind of an alcoholic and could easily make a mountain out of a molehill without even having dirt available! So, I pulled myself together and promised to call the doctor's office a few days later.

The Ghetto Practitioner

I was relieved to hear that the nodules were old, and were not moving or growing, and the doctor doubted that it was anything serious. "Nothing to worry about," he said. I ended the call and dropped to my knees, thanking God for this news and that I was finally free from the constant grip of self-doubt and fear.

The Tests

However, the search for the source of my blood loss continued. A month later, an abdominal ultrasound of my aorta came back clear—no bleeding there. But when the technician pressed the scanner over the lower right side of my abdomen, I winced in pain. I motioned to the area and mentioned the sharp discomfort, admitting that I'd been popping Tylenol like they were breath mints just to manage it. I was referred for a PET scan and sent to a gastroenterologist for the next round of tests. And so, another month of waiting began, with more tests piling up in the meantime. But my thoughts refused to settle. It was like I could see that football team forming their defensive line in my head once again, pushing against me. The thought of drinking was still far off in the distance. I knew getting drunk wouldn't make anything better.

I hadn't yet found a trusted friend in this unfamiliar town (and real friendship takes time), and now Tarry and the crew had stopped working at Brown Manor. The absence left a hollow feeling, especially with the unsettling news that I was leaking blood somewhere in my body. Thank God I have The Club and church to keep me grounded.

Brown Manor and my mission mixed into my ever-spinning thoughts. Maybe I need to make it a nonprofit so no matter what happens to me, the project will continue?

Sitting at my favorite spot at the dining table, I became hyper-aware of every little ache and pain in my body. *What if I pass out at home one day and no one finds me? I mean, how many flies would it take to finish me off?*

The football game raged on in my mind, the fans in the bleachers screaming, "Kill the quarterback!" It was all part of my stinking thinking playing out in my head, feeding my anxiety and fears. This wasn't healthy, so I called in the referee to blow the whistle. I prayed for relief, asking God to intervene and calm the storm in my mind. As always, He came through, and I was able to fall asleep that night, finding some measure of peace. But even as I rested, I knew the real challenge was still ahead of me.

Chapter Seven
RELINQUISHING

The morning of my PET Tumor Imaging Scan arrived. I awoke worried and afraid. Not knowing the future can be nerve-wracking, even in the face of my conviction that nothing happens in God's world by mistake. I hit my knees and prayed. In spite of the comfort of my routine, I still couldn't shake off that feeling of unease. Throughout the night, Mr. Insomnia was having a field day with my head, and with the constant pain in my side, that tired feeling never seemed to leave me. My morning Folgers couldn't undo this exhaustion, and I found myself falling asleep on the couch. *Maybe it's just working the night shift that is messing with my body,* I thought. *That would be great.* If it was only that simple. I forced myself to get ready and headed to the hospital.

All right, let me break this down for you. Position Emission Tomography—yes, that's the full name for a PET scan. Fancy, right? It's a diagnostic test that uses a machine to capture images of your body by detecting radiation from the emission of positrons. Now, before you start imagining a sci-fi movie, let me explain: positrons are tiny particles that come from a radioactive substance they inject into you. Sounds a bit scary, but hang with me. You'll lie on this bed, and it slides you into a big circular drum that rotates around you, snapping pictures of your internal organs. To obtain a clearer view of the organs, they'll inject a small amount of radioactive dye into your system—just enough to give everything a little glow. Don't worry, it's not enough to make you glow-in-the-dark.

Given my history with syringes, I was no stranger to IVs. Unfortunately, that same history made it harder for them to find a vein to insert the catheter. Thank God for modern technology and the two-stick rule (if they can't find a vein after two tries, they have to try a different method). In my case, the nurses had to bring in the ultrasound machine to locate a suitable vein. The best spot turned out to be on the inside of my right upper arm, just below my armpit.

During the scan, I had to keep my arms above my head—thank God for deodorant! I also had to lower my pants to my knees for the procedure. I couldn't help but smile as I remembered my mom's old scolding: "Always wear clean underwear—you never know when you might need them!"

They administered the radioactive fluid, and it gave me warm fuzzies from head to toe as I shifted back and forth on the table. The click-clacking of the machine echoed as it circled my body, capturing images. The procedure went off without a hitch. Later that week, I received a call from the doctor and went in for a visit. Of course, my mind said, "All they want is money, and this is why I am having so many visits and tests." The results from the PET scan were explained, showing significant activity in my lower right abdomen. I would have to wait for the colonoscopy to find out what had absorbed so much of the contrast. I took this news with a grain of salt and went home with no more answers than before. The only thing I could do was to give it all over to God.

Expiration Date

As much as I hate to admit it, everything that exists is temporary. All of us who grow must, one day, go. It's the reality we all live with, whether we acknowledge it or not, that everything has an expiration date. And lately, my head has been whispering that mine is approaching sooner than I'd like to think. I don't know the exact day or time; only God holds that knowledge. But I know it's coming. It's inevitable.

Education has taught me that within this mass of cells that make up who I am, there's a process called apoptosis, the molecular steps that lead a cell to its death. And who's to say it hasn't already begun? Daily, I feel that gnawing pain in my side, a reminder of whatever is wrong inside me. Three years now, it has lingered near my kidney area, and Motrin no longer helps. I could throw money at this, keep pumping meds into my system to artificially keep things going for a little longer. But we all know how the healthcare system works, and if not, welcome to the crash course.

Glancing into the rearview mirror of my life, it feels as though the Grim Reaper has been tailing me for as long as I can remember. Guns have been pulled on me, knives too. I've overdosed on drugs more times than I care to count, fallen off a car, choked on an orange, flown off a cliff in a car, and even woke up in a bed of glass after someone took an axe to the truck window where my head was resting. After surviving all that, I always thought I was invincible. But now, here I am, facing something that might finally be the end, quietly happening inside me. It's as if my body, this fragile vessel, is finally catching up to all the times I cheated death. Maybe all those close calls weren't accidents after all; maybe they were just me getting a little extra time. And now? Now it feels like the clock is ticking, and there's no escaping it.

Maybe after all these years, I have reached *my* expiration date?

Hidden

Time moves forward just the same as if it is some paragraph in a book. Thoughts of my mother, Jeanette, passing away from cancer, nagged me. The fear of the unknown gets the best of me, and I don't know what to do about it. I have reached out to several individuals to come hang out with me, never telling them I am afraid to be by myself. How do you even approach someone with this type of situation? The response is basically the same: the women I ask think that I want to date them, and the guys think it's a good way to hangout long enough to extract money from me, then leave when I tell them no. Never in my life have I felt the need to be one-hundred percent honest with people. I want to say, "I am scared, really scared." Instead, I stay silent. All my life I have been alone, and in the end it may be the same. I am blessed that I can at least share this fear with you, who turned the pages of this book you hold in your hands. Sometimes a little bit of something is better than a whole lot of nothing. No one really knows how much I suffer in silence, but it's not like I haven't felt this way before. It's just harder now. Harder to keep it all inside.

Light shines on my hidden fears, exposing them for all to see. There's no turning back now. Once you shine the light of reason on something, you can no longer allow yourself the luxury of ignorance in order to hide from it. There's nothing you can do to rewind time, so why carry the weight of it into today?

This leads to thoughts of some unresolved issues with my mother Jeanette. I used to rationalize why I felt the way I did regarding her. Maybe it's time to find the courage to confront those feelings, time to deal with something that has been holding me back.

The Day

The day of my endoscopy and colonoscopy had finally arrived. It was one of those procedures that required sedation, so I needed someone to drive me there and bring me back. I called my friend Kay, even though I knew she wasn't a morning person, and asked if she could help me. To my relief, she agreed. As we drove, I kept everything to myself.

After the procedure, I was wheeled into the recovery room, still groggy from the anesthesia. The doctor came in with the results. Kay was sitting there by my side and all I could think of was, *I hope she hadn't seen me naked* (I'm sure she was glad, too). She was calm and composed, while the doctor delivered the news.

He explained that there was no bleeding in my upper gastrointestinal (GI) tract, which brought a brief smile to my face. But then he dropped the bomb: they had found an abnormal growth in my lower GI and had taken a biopsy. He handed me a picture of what they saw in my colon. "Was this the cause of my anemia?" I asked, hoping for good news. He nodded. On the ride home, I made Kay swear not to tell anyone what the doctor had said, and she gave me her word that she wouldn't. Once I got home, I thanked her, then went inside, sat down, and opened the folder they gave me at discharge. My eyes kept drifting back to the picture of the lesion. As I stared at it, memories of my days teaching at the college flooded my mind.

When I taught first-semester nursing science at Cypress College, I always stressed to my students during the oncology section that when a lesion is discovered, we never tell the patient outright that it is cancerous. To many, the word "cancer" carries the weight of a death sentence, and that knowledge can be a heavy burden. It's devastating news to receive, but the only way to truly know what you're dealing with is through biopsy and testing. In all my years working in healthcare, I had come across many lesions and spots on patient charts, but it was always the doctor's job to break the news. My role was to help patients navigate the emotional and mental turmoil that inevitably followed, helping them process whatever the doctor told them. I guess it was my turn now to have the doctor tell me the news.

The News

The doctor scheduled an in-person meeting with me on July 22, 2024, at 3:05 p.m. As I walked into his office, a knot tightened in my stomach. He had me sit down, and as he spoke, I could barely focus on his words. He told me that the biopsy had confirmed I had invasive adenocarcinoma, or colon cancer. The next step would be more testing to determine if it had metastasized (spread) to any other parts of my body. I sat there in silence; I felt numb and couldn't think of anything to say. As I write this, I wish I was writing about someone else instead. I have already written a book about living in addiction, about homelessness, incarceration, education, and about a host of other things, and now, I am writing about having to deal with a cancer diagnosis. I guess this library of life just keeps growing.

I remained quiet for a few more minutes as his words sank in. When I finally spoke, I told the doctor, "Just leave it; let it grow." In my mind, I thought, *I am tired of being alone, and if I let it grow, I will no longer be by myself in Heaven. I am right with God and at least I won't have to watch the news anymore. Society seems to be going downhill fast, and I am tired of it all, anyway. Why fight it? Why not let God take me home? I've done enough in this life. Maybe it's time to rest.*

"I'm sixty-two years old," I said, my voice quiet but firm. "I've lived my life, and I've had a blast doing it. Maybe the best thing to do now is just let the cancer take its course and be done with it. My time has come. I have cancer."

The doctor listened without interrupting, his demeanor calm and understanding. I could tell he had been down this road before. He spoke gently, suggesting I take a few days to think it over. But in that moment, the only thought that occupied my mind was, *Okay, now what's next?*

I left the doctor's office with the oncologist's referral in hand and thought about it all the way home. Many things flowed through my head that day. Thoughts ranging from *why not just do drugs again and get drunk? I'm going to die anyway, I should just blow all my money because I cannot take it with me.* I cried a few times and wondered if any of this was worth it anymore. Then I went upstairs, said my prayers, and lay down to sleep.

Looking into the Closet

I still had some unfinished business here on this planet—something psychologically suppressed within me, causing me to feel emotionally stunted and needed further investigation. My friend, Aeli, mentioned once that maybe something from my childhood, something tied to my relationship with my mother, was behind these emotions I couldn't escape. That made me think. At the time, I dismissed it, but now, with everything crumbling around me, I couldn't ignore it any longer. It wasn't easy, but I knew I had to take a hard look at the truth. I had to confront the parts of myself I'd spent my whole life running from. So, I boldly ventured where few wish to travel—into the dark closet of my past, shining a flashlight on old fears. And there, in those suppressed memories, I found the truth I was searching for. I had to look past the fear, the anger, the denial, just so I could see things as they really were. I actually had an unresolved resentment against my mother.

It wasn't something I had wanted to admit, but there it was, clear as day. The hurt, the disappointment, the years of unspoken words—all of it had been festering, quietly shaping the person I had become.

My mother, Jeanette Joan Brown, was born into a world that didn't offer many options for a single Black woman. I now realize she did the best she could with what she knew about raising four children by herself. She did this living in the roughest of areas, where crime and violence were part of everyday life. She didn't have much support and depended on the social system to help her get by. She worked several jobs just to make sure we always had a roof over our heads and something to eat. I recall many times seeing her crying, but I never knew why. The memories of her hugging us when we were scared and scolding us when we were misbehaving flooded my consciousness. I imagine she worried about us when she had to leave the house, unsure of what she would come back to. But every time she did return, there was always food in her hands. In her brokenness, she still gave us the one thing she could: security in a most uncertain world. And now, as I reflect on it all, I feel a deep sorrow—for the pain she carried alone, for the sacrifices she made without question. But I also feel gratitude, because even though she struggled, she never gave up on us.

As a child, I was young and selfish, constantly complaining about the clothes she had to scrape together for us. Yet, I can never recall a time when we didn't have something to wear. Now, with the lens of time, I realize the sacrifices she made for us to have what we needed. It was only later, when I struggled with my own demons, that I understood how alcohol might have been her way of dulling the emotional pain she must have carried. I know this because I did the same thing in my own early adulthood. She taught me how to protect myself physically, mentally, emotionally, and socially. I learned how to fight, brush things off, keep feelings in check, and how to work hard for a living. Above all, she taught me that God was there, and that it was up to me to find Him and decide what to do once I did.

It's strange how everything changes when you sense that your time is slipping away. Things that once felt certain suddenly seem fragile and uncertain. The lessons you thought you'd mastered now demand to be revisited, examined, and fully understood. You question what truly matters, wondering what you wish you had grasped sooner. What once felt like clarity now feels like a distant, blurry memory.

As I dug through the clutter in my closet, it kicked up dust in my face, stinging my eyes. Tears welled up, but I let them come. You see, as an adult, I never got to tell my mother that I loved her. In truth, I barely spoke to her at all because I was too consumed with my addiction. Now, all I have are faint memories fading as I try to sort through them. The emotional pain surfaced, and this time, I welcomed it. I needed it. I had to feel the hurt in order to heal. It was time to uncover, discover, and discard the painful truths, no matter how hard it was. I had to admit that, for a long time, I blamed her for what happened in our home when I was a child. When she called me, just days before her death, and told me she was dying, I was in denial. Then came the final call—the one that told me she was gone. I'll never forget that empty feeling, but I had enough drugs to suppress my emotions—enough to fly the 3,000 miles back to Michigan, then return to California and spend the next years in oblivion, a shell of a person.

I continue to sift through the thoughts of what my mother must have been going through. Until now, I had kept that part of my life locked away inside. But now, as I open the door, the flood of memories rushes out. After long shifts at the hospital, my mother would come home, kick off her shoes, rub her tired feet, and then head straight into the kitchen to prepare our next meal. I remember my sisters and I eagerly waiting by her side whenever she baked a cake. She'd hand me the wooden spoon to lick, or I'd wrestle with one of my sisters to get the bowl with the remnants of batter. I can still feel the warmth of those moments. The shared birthday cakes, the hidden Christmas presents discovered under the bed—those small, precious memories brought a smile to my face as they resurfaced.

As I continued to search through the clutter of that long-closed closet, the good times emerged like sunlight piercing through the clouds, gradually making the bad times fade into the background. The truth began to rise, as if it were a new dawn, and for the first time, I saw it clearly. I understood. I finally accepted that I had been blessed with the greatest mother, the best in the whole wide world.

Jeanette Joan Saffold Brown passed away from colon cancer at fifty-three.

Chapter Eight
DISCOVERING

God's Will

That night, after cleaning out my closet, I slept deeply, waking with an unexpected sense of peace. As always, before my feet even touched the ground, I knelt and asked God to guide my thoughts. I talked with Him as I usually did, but this time, I also shared my diagnosis, asking for clarity on His will for me and the strength to embrace it. Once I finished praying, I sat back against the bed, eyes closed, feeling His presence around me. A gentle smile spread across my face, and with quiet acceptance, I whispered to myself, "Yep, I have colon cancer."

I hold to the truth that nothing happens in God's world by mistake, so as I faced cancer, my answer for today was acceptance. He's already prepared me in ways I hadn't even realized, equipping me for this journey ahead. I understand that not everyone shares my belief in God, and that's okay. I have been down that road once upon a time myself. For me, knowing and understanding God has been a process, and with time, patience, and persistence, my belief has grown stronger. Just like anything, with practice, you gain a better understanding of things, then it becomes second nature.

Without a shadow of a doubt, I believe I was led to Ohio to help homeless people with Brown Manor, a demanding project that, somehow, I was prepared for without even realizing it. When I arrived in Mansfield, a job came to me almost effortlessly, and I settled in without the financial worries that often accompany a fresh start. I had always made it a point to pay my bills on time, living by the principles I learned at The Club, to be fully self-supportive and self-sufficient. Throughout my life, I worked hard and was fortunate enough to earn my nursing license, which gave me the freedom to work anywhere in the country. Selling my house in California, with enough profit to fully pay for a home in Ohio and buy a new car, felt like everything was falling into place, as if it was all part of a plan I hadn't fully understood until now.

It seems my path was paved to prepare me for such a time as this: a comfortable retirement, complete with a pension that guarantees steady income and health insurance for the rest of my life, and the blessing of a compassionate, understanding new boss like Crystal. The blend of financial stability and the support of someone who truly cares has given me the freedom to take the time I need to focus on my health and navigate this new challenge. In all of this, I can't help but see God's hand at work, guiding me to this moment when I needed it most.

I was clearly told by God that I am never allowed to harbor hate for anyone—which eases the frustration that comes with this diagnosis. I was also told never to intentionally harm another, which prevents me from displacing my fears onto others through anger. And perhaps most important, He told me I am always to finish what I start. This means that, in working on Brown Manor, I must find a new revenue stream.

After much thought about what I discovered in my closet, I realized the best way I could honor my mother's legacy was to establish the JJSF—Jeanette Joan Saffold Foundation. In her name, I will partner with many others to create a nonprofit organization dedicated to refurbishing abandoned properties and transforming them into homes for those living on the streets. Between this project and the book, I've found enough to keep my mind occupied, leaving little room to worry about cancer.

The more I think about it, the more I realize how blessed I am to be here. And God is still in the miracle business, so I am exactly where I need to be. And there is nothing He brings me to that He won't help me through.

Choices

Reality is one strange place to live, and with each passing day, it only gets more bizarre. In life, choices are inevitable—like when I chose to eat an entire pizza in one sitting. I have made the choice to come to Ohio, to finish Brown Manor, to face cancer.

Kay once told me I was spoiled after I casually mentioned that I once hired other people to handle my basic needs. And Jim, my sponsor, called me a sexist when I said the only reason to get married was so someone could do the laundry, clean the house, and cook meals. He made me swear to *never* let that be my approach to marriage. I guess my understanding of marriage needed a little tweaking. My feelings were a bit hurt at the time, but I listened. I did my laundry, stayed single, and for fifteen years, I hired a housekeeper instead. Not quite what Jim had in mind, but hey, it worked for me.

I was never much of a shopper either, but I remember my friend John—"Boochie," we called him—with his thick New York accent, was a shopping maestro. He always knew where the best sales were and was never without a coupon. I used to have him handle all my clothes shopping for me. Then there was David—practically a fashionista. This guy knew *everything* about style. I swear, he's the only person I've ever met who could make a rubber chicken look like high fashion. It didn't matter what their personal beliefs or lifestyles were; the best decision I ever made was making those two guys my friends. Thanks to them, I always look sharp.

Choices are something we all make in life. Sort of like, "Do you want to *enter* something or do you want to *exit* something?" Even if you choose not to do either, you have still made a choice. I chose to follow Jim's direction, and it kept me sober. I chose to put this book into your hands—the one you are reading now—so you can understand why I do what I do. I chose to believe that a Power greater than myself could restore me to sanity, and I also choose to turn my will and life over to Him. I made this choice because of what I was given years ago. So now I come at a fork in the road; how should I deal with this cancer and the outcome? I have that choice, don't I?

With Boochie and David, all I had to do was tell them where I needed to go or what event I had to attend, and they would make sure I had what I needed for the occasion. When it came to housekeeping, Berta was the best. After she passed away, her husband and kids stepped in to handle things around the house. Toward the end of my time in California, my friend Grassy pitched in with cleaning and meal prep, as did my neighbor Sara. Life was good, and I had built a routine where most things were taken care of for me.

But now, everything has shifted. I'm faced with a new choice—perhaps the biggest one yet in this thing called life. The choice is simple: Do I want to live, or will I let myself die?

Chapter Nine
SEYMOUR

Seymour

With this new cancer diagnosis, I found myself standing at a crossroads: I could either deny it or accept it. Considering my background in nursing, I knew what was happening inside me was just a bunch of cells throwing a tantrum and going rogue. Honestly, at this point, I should have earned a PhD in dealing with rebellious behavior—I've certainly had my share of it over the years! However, I decided not to allow myself any negative thinking about some odd monster currently taking up residence in my body.

With my coffee mug in hand, I took a sip and prayed. The decision came to deal with this head on, without hesitation. From this point forward, I would work with my doctors and follow the next steps they laid out before me. I took another sip and prayed some more. This thought came into my head: *since the cancer is in the cecum portion of my intestines, I'll name him Seymour. Seymour of the Cecum! A groovy name.* I decided to treat him like I would treat any sick friend—check in, offer support, and politely but firmly show him the door when it was time. Seymour didn't seem all that frightening now.

The Ghetto Practitioner

All right, so now that Seymour had officially moved in, I had to figure out what to do with him.

Since God was steering this bus, I might as well sit back and see where the ride would take me. But riding the bus all by myself isn't much fun, so I reached out to a friend of mine and shared the news. I called Drew and told him about my new uninvited houseguest, Seymour. Drew agreed Seymour must go. He also agreed that we must serve Seymour an eviction notice—immediately. Then, in classic Drew fashion, he sent me the video from *Little Shop of Horrors* with the song "Feed Me, Seymour." I couldn't help but laugh out loud. Leave it to the good doctor to know exactly how to lift my spirits when I need it most.

Now that I had my marching orders, and a snazzy theme song, it was time to meet the surgeon who would help kick Seymour to the curb.

Meet the Surgeon

A few days later, I met my surgical oncologist, Dr. Sheth, a kind man who instantly put me at ease. After a few minutes of friendly conversation, he ordered a series of new tests so we could map out a plan. He ordered a full CT scan with contrast to make sure Seymour hadn't packed his bags and started squatting in any other parts of my body. I mean, I know Seymour's type: give them an inch, and next thing you know, they're redecorating the whole place! And in this case, if I let him stay too long, he wouldn't just take over my life—he'd *take* my life.

It was during that visit I informed the good doctor I had christened my cancer, Seymour. He just smiled and told me another patient of his had named a cyst, so it wasn't all that uncommon.

Who knew?

With a long list of potential treatments, my focus narrowed quickly. *How was I going to pay for all this? What was I supposed to do about Brown Manor now?*

Worry started creeping in. I reached out for help, asking others if they could step up and volunteer. But even with extra hands, the work had come to a grinding halt. I asked JR from the Blue Rose Foundation to lend a hand—and bless them, they did—but I still had to wrestle with the city for building permits.

Now my concerns were piling up: Brown Manor's future, money and, of course, Seymour. This time, I just cried and went to sleep.

A month later, the CT scan was scheduled, followed by a visit with the surgeon a few days after that. "Good news," Dr. Sheth said, offering a smile. Seymour had only settled in the cecum, and since he was staying put, surgery became the best option to remove it. At first, I thought my choices were limited to either "regular" (doing nothing) or "extra crispy" (chemo or radiation). But it turned out the best way to deal with Seymour was The Ginsu! The plan was for Dr. Sheth to slice Seymour right out of there, taking all the surrounding lymph tissue with him. Afterward, they'd measure the CEA levels to check for any signs of trouble.

"Would I have to have a colostomy bag?" I asked, as disturbing body images came to mind. Dr. Sheth reassured me, saying he didn't think that would be necessary. I felt a wave of relief and thanked him.

Things are not always cut and dried, so of course, the good doctor told me he would first need to look at Seymour once he was inside, and biopsy the surrounding lymph tissue to determine if chemotherapy would be needed afterwards. My mind quickly went to *maybe chemo will fry my innards, which may or may not extend my time here on this planet. However, just letting Seymour take its course will eventually kill me. The question is: do I want to arrive at the pearly gates regular or extra crispy?*

He gave me the chance to ask as many questions as I wanted, which I appreciated. He explained the options for surgery: he could go with the old-fashioned approach and just cut me open to give Seymour the boot, or he could try the less invasive methods—make a few tiny holes (laparoscopy), or let a robot do the surgery. The latter two would require me to be under anesthesia longer, and the less time I spent under, the better for my respiratory system. So, I chose the old school method—slice me up like I was some good old-fashioned welfare bologna!

I asked one last question: once he removed Seymour, could I take him home in a bottle of formaldehyde and ask him why he was trying to kill me? He politely replied, "No," explaining that it was illegal to keep body parts in your home—although, later I learned that wasn't exactly true; there's no law against it. "Could I at least have a picture of Seymour?" I grinned. He agreed to that. Of course, I had to ask if he would sign the picture, but he just laughed.

More tests came in. I thought Seymour was just a tiny tot of tissue, but then I saw my carcinoembryonic antigen (CEA) levels were sky-high—in the 90s—when they should've been under five. It seemed Seymour was definitely showboating, trying to make sure everyone knew he was there. I also found out he was a legitimate Stage IIIB (T3 N1) cancer. With that kind of street cred, I'm honestly surprised he went unnoticed for this long.

I've come to accept Seymour as my sidekick—literally, he's inside, on my right side—until the doctor evicts him. I had this wild thought that I could take him home and have a little heart-to-heart. After all, with my medical background, I know the best way to get the truth is from the source, right? So, wouldn't it be beneficial to have a face-to-face chit-chat with Seymour and hear what he had to say? I shared this idea with my longtime friend Debbie, and she looked at me like I was crazy. Then, just to add a bit of humor, I mentioned I'd lost some weight through all of this and maybe, after the operation, I should look into getting some booty implants. Her response was priceless: "Now I know there's something seriously wrong with you."

Moving Forward

I've spent years learning how to prepare someone for surgery and handle their post-op care. I'm skilled in wound sutures and have seen it all, but have never been *the patient* of an operation before. That, however, was about to change. I couldn't help but wonder what other cancer patients think when they first receive their diagnosis. There are support groups for just about everything in this world, and I'm no stranger to seeking help from that arena. After all, that's part of why I went to The Club and sat in church basements.

But this illness? It felt different. It was almost embarrassing to me. I let few people know. But it was eating at me; I needed to talk to someone. Then, as if by magic, out of the corner of my eye, I saw him. The one I trusted more than anyone, sitting on the table, patiently waiting. His blue fur was a bit ruffled, his bow tie crooked—my stuffed, blue best friend, always there to listen and keep my secrets safe.

I pulled Bunny closer, telling him I had come to terms with Seymour and had a plan in place. Some serious thinking had to happen, though. Being an addict isn't something that's just in the past; it's always there. And with surgery, narcotics are part of the deal. There's a whole buffet of pain medications out there, and for someone like me, drugs are like potato chips: one is too many, and a thousand is never enough! The surgery ahead of me meant an opportunity for pain meds to be handed out like Skittles.

"And with the seriousness of Seymour," I told him, "and having good insurance, I'd be eligible for the full smorgasbord of goodies!"

Bunny sat quietly, staring with his soft, unblinking eyes. Knowing how good a listener he was, I felt safe to continue. "When my mother, Jeanette, had cancer, I was so consumed by my addiction that at her funeral, after a brief introduction to the family I hadn't seen in ten years, I shamefully and pathetically went straight to her bathroom to rummage through the medicine cabinets and see if they'd forgotten to 'properly dispose of' her pain meds."

The rabbit stared blankly, without judgment, as if to say, "It's okay. The past is the past. What mattered now was what I chose to do. After all, all we really have is today."

I know all too well that addiction is cunning, baffling, and powerful. Was I willing to give up twenty-five years of sobriety? If I released that genie from the bottle, my life as I knew it would be over. The simple thought of having a glass of morphine with a twist of lemonade would land me in jail, where I'd probably die from some infection, unable to follow proper aftercare directions (I had to play the tape all the way through).

Then I smiled, rubbed my abdomen, and said aloud for Seymour to hear, "That was a good one." Bunny sat still, without saying a word. I gave him a nod of thanks and said, "I guess I am ready to move forward now."

Chapter Ten
RESULTS

The Edge

I wish I could say knowing God is in charge keeps me from the edge, but I still dangle at times. Having Seymour as an uninvited guest has made for a rollercoaster of emotions. Pity and sympathy aren't what I need. Maybe that's why I've kept this battle to myself. However, since I will be disappearing for a few days for my surgery, accountability was a must.

When I told my boss, Crystal, she was understanding but pointed out that my coworkers would be curious about what had happened to me. I told her I'd fill them in when the time felt right. Maybe they won't find out until they read this book, just like everyone else. Becky, a cancer survivor and acquaintance of mine, knows. Of course, Debbie knows, too. She's my oldest friend and my rock. I also had to tell my roommate, since I'll likely need her help during recovery. And then there's Kay, who was there when I came out of my colonoscopy. This little group of insiders was growing.

And now, here you are reading these words, so you've made it into my inner circle as well. Welcome.

I know sharing all this will bring a symphony of condolences and prayer offers. While I appreciate the gestures, I trust God knows exactly what He's doing, and I've left it all in His hands. I even hesitated talking this over with Bunny. I mean, with his temper, I could just imagine him wanting to climb up my behind and take on Seymour himself, which would leave me in an extremely awkward position!

Standing on the edge always brings a choice: either look down into the abyss of despair or up into the stars of hope. I know the best choice is to stay focused on the present. For a few minutes, I had the pleasure of some insane thinking. Like, I could go out and buy a crack rock the size of a melon, smoke it out of a tuba, and live out the fantasy I once had. Or I could stop all my projects, grow a beard, and escape from myself. But the problem with that is, no matter where I go, I'd still be taking me with me.

I could just abandon Brown Manor, give it away, let the foundation be donated to another cause. I could sell my house, grab Bunny, and go on a wild road trip in a Winnebago until we run out of money, then end up living in a shelter for people who talk to stuffed animals...until Seymour grows large enough to do me in.

You know, just your average Manic Monday type of thoughts.

All these options flow through my head, even the thought of asking God to take me home. After all, He answers prayers, doesn't He? I've seen it with my own eyes, that when a person is near the end, they hang on just long enough to say their goodbyes, and then they let go. I remember when my brother Kevin, who found me years after I left home, told me Jeanette was dying. She called me. I can still hear her raspy voice saying, "Tony, I am dying," followed by those words I'd never heard from her before—"I love you." That was the first time she spoke to me as an adult, and the last time she ever spoke to me again. Two days later, my sister called to tell me that Mom had passed. I believe Jeanette waited just to hear my voice once more before she let life go.

Maybe I could ask God for that one favor, to say good-bye, and then let me come home to Heaven. Life, and the world around me, doesn't hold the same appeal now that Seymour is here.

Finish What You Start

And what about Brown Manor? I have to finish what I started—Seymour or no Seymour. Someone once reached out to help me when I had nothing, and because of that, I've been given the chance to serve others. This is why I'm here, and this is what drives me. We are our brothers' and sisters' keepers, aren't we? All that I possess doesn't mean a thing if I turn away from those in need now.

Brown Manor still has a long way to go. Neglected for ages, it was left to decay and stripped bare. The copper pipes were stolen, along with anything else of value. As a kid, I did my fair share of "scrapping" pipes, hauling them off to the junkyard for some quick cash. I wonder if this is what "what goes around comes around" means. What do they say about payback?

What wasn't stolen from the house had been ravaged by the changing seasons, leaving much of it in such disrepair that almost everything had to be replaced or brought up to modern codes. I could feel the weight of responsibility on my shoulders, growing heavier with the thought. The good news was, I didn't have time to think about Seymour.

My finances were running low—fast. I had once proclaimed, "It's not my money, but God's, and I'm meant to use it to help others." But I wouldn't live forever. I had no clue back then that Seymour would make an unexpected entrance into my life.

The edge forced my direction—to seek refuge. So, I looked up at the stars and had another heart-to-heart with God, something I'd done countless times before. And, as always, the answer came. Though, in a way I never could've imagined.

I was sitting in my favorite spot, with my back to the window that faced the front of the house. My eyes closed, and I prayed. "God, how am I going to pay for everything that needs to be done?"

He answered in His own unmistakable way, and much faster than usual. I suppose He knew how much I was hurting. His response came clear and direct: *"With the money you have."*

I hesitated and replied, "But God, why do I have to use the money that I have? So little is left."

He answered gently, *"When you were born, you had no money; when you were homeless, you had no money; and when you die, you'll have no money. All that you have is Mine, so use it."*

I then asked, "But God, if I use all the money on Brown Manor, what will I have left?"

He said, *"Your house is paid for, your car is paid for; you have a nursing license in two states, and a secure job. What else do you need?"*

Well, I couldn't really argue with that. And besides, God always wins anyway. So, I surrendered and said, "Thanks." I made a commitment right then and there to use all the money I had saved in my accounts for Brown Manor.

Less than five minutes after I made that promise, my Ring doorbell went off. I pulled up the camera on my phone, and there, right in front of my house, was a family of deer—just feasting on my flowers. One deer looked up at the doorbell, while another stared straight at me.

I bowed my head and cried. I knew, without a doubt, I had made the right decision.

When God says, "Yes," I've learned to brace myself and tie my shoestrings up tight. Since that night, donations have been pouring in for Brown Manor. A local lumber company, Richland Lumber, generously donated drywall. I met with the owner, Jason, one day over a cup of coffee, and he told me he wanted to make a difference. Since then, the drywall has kept coming.

The Blue Rose Foundation stepped in with more drywall, insulation, and labor. JR spearheaded their contributions, and Kokosing Asphalt pledged to donate materials and labor for our parking lot. Tiffany and Lee offered to cover all the asphalt costs. Home Depot generously provided supplies for the bathrooms and kitchen, and Jamie from Monarch Countertops donated countertops. Narda and Brandon Greter from Prima Visual Media donated a 3D virtual walkthrough of the house and provided us with blueprints of the property.

We've also received furniture, gift certificates, and a team of volunteers eager to help with Brown Manor. All this happened because of that one conversation with God. Thinking about it fills me with such gratitude that I want to have another chit-chat with Him, just to express my thanks.

It's amazing how God invests His resources when all I had to do was make a small down payment. This is His way of reminding me, in no uncertain terms, that He is still in charge. I began to think deeper about the bigger picture. My unexpected journey, the donations, the new opportunities, they weren't just coincidences. They were part of a larger plan. But this movie was just getting started, so I had to stay put and watch it until the end.

Chapter Eleven
PRACTICE

Thinking

I have a tendency to overthink—perhaps too much, as some might say. Today is no different. In fact, my mind is in hyperdrive most of the time! The sound of Beethoven's "Für Elise" plays softly in the background, and I am taking things in stride, just waiting for the day of surgery. But tomorrow, I may completely fall apart. On those days, I sleep a lot, with no energy to do much of anything. Fear of another fainting episode plays a part in that. Could it happen again?

With a day off from work, I'll head to the club or church to gather enough strength to keep my head up. Seymour will, for now, remain a close-knit secret because people tend to get all sad over things like this. Perhaps those, not knowing what to say to a person in my situation, may shy away from me, creating the pain of isolation, leading to rejection.

My thoughts drift back to Jeanette. I realize now how harshly I judged her, shaped by my own upbringing. But given the circumstances she faced, I know she did the best she could with what she had. She gave birth to me before civil rights were even a reality for her. Looking back on her life, and everything she accomplished on her own, a touch of sadness comes over me. She was a nurse before she died, and now, years later, here I am, a nurse too, with cancer. I guess I'm more like her than I ever realized.

Lexie continued playing another tune by Ludwig while I sat at my favorite place at the table. Hyperactive bowels have plagued me and once relieved, I noticed red blood on the toilet paper. This was something new for me. I tried to distract myself by reading something, but the unsettling sound of my bowels stirred again. I returned to the bathroom—again, more blood. Feeling weaker, I decided to drive myself to the emergency room. I got in the car, and in my best Fred Sanford impression, muttered to myself, "Jeanette, I'm coming to join you."

Once at the ER, I waited to be seen. The doctor arrived and examined me by running his hands over my abdomen and listening to my concerns. After a moment, he looked up and said, "Yes, you're bleeding internally." *Maybe God has answered me and it was time for me to go.* The doctor suggested admitting me, but I shook my head. I wanted to go home. A surgeon from my doctor's group was there and consulted with her for a second opinion. I waited quietly, watching the IV fluids slowly drip into my veins. Half an hour later, he returned. Since my surgery was scheduled for the following week, I could go home for now, but I needed to contact my surgeon the next day. I agreed, took the prescribed iron tablets, and left for home.

Is There a Doctor in the House?

Once home, I threw the best pity party that a person could have. *It is true now; I am finally dying.* I sat in my favorite place and asked Lexie to play anything. "Lean On Me" by Bill Withers filled the room. Physically drained, and so tired of everything, I curled up on the sofa. Defeated, I cried myself to sleep. As always, sleep didn't last long, and once again, I was left with my thoughts, staring at the ceiling.

I thought about what it's like to have an advanced degree in nursing and not have the time to use it. A nurse practitioner is almost like a doctor, and with the current health care professional shortage, nurse practitioners fill in the gap. I could do something about it. Even if I never practice under that specific license, at least I can say that no matter where you come from or your past, anything is possible. I truly want to help those in the community who can't afford the health care services they need. A smile found my lips. I really could be *The Ghetto Practitioner.* All my accumulated experiences from all the doctors I have practiced under could help to make the world a better place. That is indeed something worth living for.

This spurred memories of some of the groovy doctors I wanted to grow up to be like, people like Dr. Drew Pinsky and Dr. Stone from Cornerstone in Southern California. Dr. Stone was the first person to give me a chance when I started in healthcare. With his cool British accent and genuine warmth, he had a way of connecting with people. He cared deeply about his clients and taught me so much about addiction medication and detoxing people the old-fashioned way—with Robaxin, clonidine, ibuprofen, and just a little bit of Ativan. That's how we used to treat opiate addiction detox back then. We were also part of some of the first controlled study groups for Suboxone when it was first introduced. Dr. Stone was at the helm, guiding us through it. Those early experiences shaped my understanding of addiction and treatment in ways I never imagined, and I've always carried them with me.

Dr. Choi was another favorite and one of the best psychiatrists I've ever had the pleasure of working with. He had this quiet, calming presence, and no matter how off-track or delusional his patients were, he always took the time to listen. There was never a time when he wasn't smiling, and he made himself available to the staff, whether it was day or night. He treated all of us like we were the most important part of the team, always showing his appreciation. Every year at Christmas, he'd give us gift certificates as a thoughtful reminder of how much he valued our work. His kindness and dedication exemplified the leadership that leaves a lasting impression.

As I sat there, more and more memories of the doctors I had worked with surfaced. It was as if my mind was trying to tell me something Was it fear creeping in, disguised as nostalgia? Or was it hope, quietly making its way back into my thoughts? Whatever it was, I couldn't stop thinking about those doctors.

I couldn't help but think of Dr. Helfat, a doctor from the old school—gruff as all get out, no-nonsense, and tough as nails. But despite his rough exterior, he was an excellent teacher. He'd often let me stand beside him as he explained his reasoning behind prescribing medication for certain conditions or why he chose one treatment over another. "Cantankerous" might as well have been his middle name, but deep down, he had a heart the size of Texas. I remember the day he did Mrs. Hunt's annual physical. He looked at me with a steady gaze and told me to rush her to the hospital immediately. Mrs. Hunt had trained *me* as the director of nursing services, and she once gave me a piece of advice that stuck with me: "Either you're going to be a nice guy, or you're going to be a son-of-a-bitch. You can't be both." It's funny how those two were like peas and carrots—completely different, yet inseparable in their own way. Neither of them are with us anymore, but their influence and memories will stay with me forever.

A sharp pain shot through my side. Seymour has a way of getting my attention and putting a damper on things. My stomach began its grumbling, warning me that more bleeding was on its way. "I don't care anymore," I told myself, then shifted my position on the sofa to lessen the pain.

Why won't Seymour just leave me alone?

So many doctors have played a pivotal role in shaping who I am today. If it hadn't been for Dr. Shams, I never would have made it through the nurse practitioner program.

Dr. Ringer gifted me with the fantastic smile I now share with the world. Dr. Douliu taught me the importance of making independent decisions as a nurse supervisor, and my dear friend Arnold Franco's guidance was crucial in helping me get this far in my career. Each one of these individuals has instilled parts of themselves in me, and when I combine all those lessons, I see who I've become in the medical field. I'm deeply grateful for their love, their lessons, and their patience over the years. Without them, I wouldn't be the nurse I am today. These thoughts began to motivate me. A new sense of strength took root, and I soon felt like Popeye after devouring a can of spinach!

Suddenly, I wanted to live again. I wanted to reach for the stars and fulfill the purpose God has set for me. Beyond everything else, I owe this new drive to the doctors who dedicated their time and resources to shape me into who I am today. And now, I find myself a student once more, eager to learn and grow.

The proverbial shoe was on the other foot as I rose from the couch and headed toward the bathroom. I am the patient now, but for how long, only God knows. I truly believe this time, I'll make it. All the incredible doctors who've come into my life have taught me the most valuable lesson: we are all our brothers' and sisters' keepers. Without them, there would be no "me" to keep pushing forward, and we all have a role to play in making a difference in someone else's life. It would be a disservice to waste the knowledge and wisdom they've invested in me. There's no time for self-pity; I have work to do.

That's Not Real

The pep talk lasted only a minute, but it gave me the boost I needed. I sank back onto the sofa and said, "Lexie, play Gordon Lightfoot." The haunting notes of "The Wreck of the Edmund Fitzgerald" filled the room. When the song ended, I said, "Off," and she fell silent. I wondered if I had hurt her feelings, but then I sighed, "Oh well," and reached for the remote, eager to see what was happening in the world.

The television was created for entertainment, and I could use a little of that right now. I just needed to zone out and not think about Seymour for a while. I placed my hand on my abdomen, hoping to calm the rumbling, but it didn't help. So, I kept my eyes glued to the screen, mindlessly flipping through channels.

Something on the television took me back to my childhood, to the days when I would watch the old Superman series with George Reeves. Every time he would say, "Up, up, and awayyy," my little innocent heart would race like there was no tomorrow. I remember the fun times, running around the house with a sheet tied around my neck, repeating his words. Of course, I had to test my superpowers by leaping off the dresser onto the bed. Oh, the day Mom got upset because I had used a clean sheet to fly off the dresser! Unfortunately, I missed the bed and landed on my superhero noggin and bled all over the place. She had to use the sheet as a tourniquet to wrap around my head. I guess I wasn't really made of steel after all.

I laughed audibly as Seymour rumbled again, but this time, I didn't pay him any attention and flicked to another channel, letting my mind drift back to those carefree childhood days. That's when the image of wrestling suddenly popped into my head.

One of my favorite wrestlers back in the day was George "the Animal" Steele. This guy was a beast—literally. He'd rip the top turnbuckle off with his teeth and then bite people on the face. I was so mesmerized by his savage antics, I thought, *I want to be just like him!* So, naturally, I started channeling my inner Animal and took to biting my little sister, Alicia. She'd cry, run to Mom, so a whole "course of correction" had to be made. I wasn't stopped that easily. So, I switched to biting my older sister, Quinetta.

Well, I had severely underestimated Quinetta. One day, when I tried to bite her, she flipped the script on me. She looked me dead in the eye and said, "I'm Randy 'Macho Man' Savage." And without missing a beat, she delivered a picture perfect "flying elbow drop" off the top of the dresser onto my stomach. This not only knocked the wind out of me but also hurt like hell. That ended my belief in television wrestling. However, when it came to the big screen, that was a different story.

In Steubenville, Ohio, there was a movie theater on Fourth Street called The Grand. Ah, what a fun place that was back in the day! It was here that I saw my first Bruce Lee movie. And let me tell you, Bruce could whoop some serious butt. After the movie, I would run down the street kicking everything in sight. That worked well when my opponent was a trash can or a mailbox. Yeah, I learned the hard way that movie-style martial arts don't exactly hold up in real life when I went against a real person who was well-versed in *real* fighting. I remember taking my karate stance, but before I could get out a decent, "Hiii yaaa," my voice was silenced by a well-placed fist across the lips. Not much fun then. But thank God, anyway, for entertainment to pull me away from the realities of the moment! The smile was needed for sure, and I was grateful to turn the channel to some mindless fodder.

The rumbling in my abdomen escalated to a full-blown symphony, and I needed to do something about it. I turned off the television and just lay there for a minute, thinking. They always say, "youth is wasted on the young." And let me tell you, I *really* get that now. How fun it was being young and silly! Carefree, happy, adventurous, and tossing caution to the wind. Reckless enough to think riding downhill on a Big Wheel without a helmet was a good idea, heading toward oncoming traffic with nothing but a cheap pair of sneakers for brakes. How sad it is that we all must eventually grow up. I don't care what anybody thinks, but I really miss tearing apart a box of Honey Comb just to get the prize ring from inside.

Seymour's surgery is next week, and I am so ready to part ways with him.

Chapter Twelve
FAITH

The Parting Party

Time does what time does, and now, the time has come to have Seymour Gensu'd out of me. I have arranged with my roommate what may be needed once I return from the hospital. I have also called my friend Becky—who has walked through a similar diagnosis—several times, but I haven't heard back from her yet. I pray all is well. Ready or not, it's time for me to move forward. Although the external bleeding has subsided, I know Seymour is still in there, doing something, and soon he will be gone. I have spent more time at church and The Club recently, to be emotionally and spiritually ready for the next steps I must take. Dr. Drew and Debbie will help me stay accountable because of my addictive personality, and for the careful use of the narcotics needed for adequate pain relief.

In just a few days, strangers will cut into my abdomen, removing part of my intestine, and this rattles my peace.
In one of the first classes I took for my master's program, I learned a lifelong practice of maintaining peace, one that, at this moment, stands out to me. It was the Ten Caritas Pro-

cesses, as outlined by Dr. Jean Watson. These included practicing loving-kindness, being authentically present, honoring belief systems, developing trusting relationships, forgiving and showing empathy, growth through problem-solving and solution-seeking, engaging in teaching-learning experiences, creating a caring and healing environment, valuing humanity, and being open, allowing for miracles in life. I spent every day for months learning how to apply these principles to my world.

Peaceful Practice Within

By embracing these core principles and applying them within the medical field, I discovered a peaceful practice within myself, one that brought me closer to God and the truths in His word. It takes courage to look inward, to uncover and discard the things that block us from truly experiencing the Sunlight of the Spirit. Loving yourself enough to heal and grow is the key to feeling the love of others. When I became my own best friend, I could be a better friend to those around me. In doing so, it deepened my relationship with my Creator.

Being friendly is a no-brainer; most of us do it because it's expected and part of participating in society. But being a true friend requires the giving of oneself. There's a profound truth in the saying, "It is in the giving that we receive." However, lately this feels like a lonely one-way road I am traveling. I have many friends, but today they feel far off, merely acquaintances and associates. Today, I must be my own best friend, and the groovy part about that is, it has drawn me closer to experiencing God's love. His love is unconditional; He shows me this daily. Moving forward, I put all my trust in God. This is what faith is all about.

Faith

"Fear and faith cannot occupy the same space at the same time," or so it's said. Now, let me get a little nerdy for a moment (and indulge my inner smartypants) and share something from quantum physics. The Pauli Exclusion Principle states: "No two identical fermions (matter particles) can occupy the same quantum state." In simpler terms—two's a crowd. Fear is a primal emotional response that alerts us to potential danger, whether it's physical or psychological. Faith, however, is an active trust based on evidence. They may not "occupy" the same space, but they both can certainly shout into the room from the outside!

Now, here's where it gets important: you have a choice. You can lean into your faith and push fear into the background, cowering in the dark. Or, as some people put it, "Have faith, and if you have to, do it afraid." Or let fear lead and bully faith into the shadows. It's up to you.

Standing strong in faith has given me perseverance, and through that perseverance, I've been able to achieve some pretty incredible things on my journey. What's even cooler is that I'm not doing this alone.

If you were to ask me what the key to my success is, I'd tell you without hesitation, "My strong belief in God." Some people laugh when I say that, but I just shrug it off. When they ask me again, I smile and tell them I have a superpower. That usually gets a few more chuckles, but then I hit them with this: "I just do what people say I cannot accomplish."

You see, when I was a child, I was told I would never amount to much. But now, here you are, holding my second book in your hands. I was told I couldn't get a nursing license—now I'm a nurse practitioner. I was told I was selfish—now my life is dedicated to helping others in every way I can. And I was told God wasn't real. Well, here I am, living proof that He exists.

If I can overcome all that, so can you. The limits others set for us don't define who we are or what we're capable of. You've got the power to prove them wrong, just like I did.
I truly believe I'll make a comeback—stronger than before. Think of it like the wounded caterpillar that instinctively knows what happens once it enters the cocoon. Just like that caterpillar, I know that one day, I'll soar higher than ever before.

But here's the thing: metamorphosis is a slow process. It's not always quick or easy, but it's necessary. And God isn't done with me yet. Just like Brown Manor isn't finished, and the Jeanette Joan Saffold Foundation isn't either, there's more to come. And if He isn't done with me, He isn't done with you, either. The best IS yet to come! God never brings us to something unless He's planning to bring us through it.

The dust from my pity party began to dissipate, and the fresh air of hope took its place. Seymour's eviction notice has been served and moving day is here!

Chapter Thirteen
THE STORY

The Final Countdown

Preparations for my goodbye to Seymour have given me the pleasure of chugging a huge bottle of GoLYTELY, then taking six different antibiotics. Nothing gets the party started like downing a cocktail of gastrointestinal discomfort. Another sleepless night ahead, as Mr. Insomnia has also RSVP'd to this gala. Not a big deal, but tonight I do not have the energy to banter with him.

For those who have not had this experience, prepping for surgery is a time-consuming task. Especially if it's an intestinal operation. Before they can do anything, the "plumbing" must be thoroughly scrubbed clean. They give you this salty, sodium sulfate-based solution you must drink in eight-ounce doses every fifteen minutes over a four-hour period (that's sixteen glasses of this stuff!).

Pro Tip: Fill the container with water and place it in the refrigerator a couple of days beforehand. This will make it easier—should I say, more tolerable?—to drink. It also comes with a lemon-flavored packet to mix in, attempting to impart some kind of funky soft drink taste. But in reality, it tastes like a lemon-flavored lie.

I got that ready and waited for D-Day.

I use the term D-Day, because once you drink this stuff, you will have bowel movements *all day*—I mean, *all* day—so your system will be as clean as a whistle. Making sure there was plenty of toilet paper in the house (a lesson carried over from COVID days), and that my roommate knew what to expect, I designated the downstairs bathroom as the proverbial drop zone. For my last supper, I devoured the left-over pizza and wings from Marcos, along with half a bag of cheddar pretzel popcorn from Swavory's of downtown Mansfield. After that, all systems were go. I said a prayer, thanked God for getting me to this point, and braced myself for what would come next.

Thursday, August 29, 2024, the hospital called, reminding me that my surgery was scheduled for the next day—Friday, at 1230 hours. In my best astronaut voice, I replied, "Roger that," and hung up the phone. A sudden fear crept over me. *What if I die during surgery?* I took care of that, too, and prayed.

At 1200 hours, I stopped all eating. I drank nothing but water—no Folgers in my cup this morning. At 1400 hours, I took the first two antibiotics, and at 1500 hours, I took the second set and pulled the "Golightly" out of the fridge. At 1600 hours, I began chugging the salty concoction, and thus, Operation Blowout commenced. I'll spare you the gritty details of the battle that ensued inside, but let me just say this: if you ever find yourself facing a colon prep, be wary of coughing, sneezing, and, for the love of all things sacred, watching comedies. Trust me.

At around 0100, early Friday morning, the storm inside me subsided just enough to where I felt safe to go to bed. But Mr. I. was up to his typical tricks by asking me if I was ready to die in a few hours. I looked over at Bunny, and he gave me the "Go get 'em, Tiger" look. That made me smile, and I again prayed and asked for peace. God answered, and I went to sleep.

Surgery

Friday morning, 0900, I awoke and took a shower. The pre-op instructions were clear: no deodorant today due to "operational concerns." I thought, *Great, now I am going to smell pretty funky when I get to Heaven.* Not exactly the first impression I was hoping to make at the pearly gates.

Once dressed, I left my house for "the last mile." My roommate had her instructions: check the mail, empty the trash, and be available in case I needed a ride home from surgery. She was good with it all, and I said, "Great. That is groovy."

I was already on my way, having a little extra chit-chat with God, when I got a call from the surgery department asking if I could come in earlier. Of course, no problem—there's nothing in my life that God can't handle. I pulled into the long-term lot across the street and parked my car. Once through the hospital doors, the receptionist directed me downstairs, and from there, an attendant escorted me to the back. I was given the dreaded hospital gown (you know the one), slid into the one-size-fits-all yellow booties, and placed the light blue surgical hat on my head. I couldn't help myself and tipped the hat to the side to look cool and pimp-walked my way into surgery.

The nurses were kind and apologetic for sticking me with a needle, unaware that in an earlier chapter of my life, I had stuck myself so often that it didn't really bother me anymore.

They got the IV started, and just like every journey begins, they asked if I needed to go to the bathroom. I knew if I didn't go then and needed to later, they would have to insert a catheter. Just the thought of a Foley being inserted scared about 10 cc's of urine out of me. Then the anesthesiologist and my doctor came in, ticking off more boxes before converting the bed I was lying on into a gurney and wheeling me toward the operating theater.

Dr. Sheth was sitting behind a desk in the furthest corner of the theater, getting into his "thought zone," as they confirmed it was really me and slid me onto the operating table. The anesthesiologist said he would give me something soothing to relax me, and the next thing I knew, it was off to Snoozeville.

I Studied Medicine for This

Sedated, I was there, but wasn't *all* there. An endotracheal tube was inserted down my throat, passing anesthesia gases through it, and a soft bite block was inserted into my mouth. Completely unconscious, Seymour's eviction began. Based on the surgery notes and my knowledge in the medical field, this is a summation of the events: a Foley catheter was inserted anyway, and I was shaved from my diaphragm down to my pelvis. My belly was now as smooth as my buttocks! Then they cleansed the area with some type of Betadine solution (I am referring to the belly—stay focused readers). Once cleansed, a sterile drape was applied across my abdomen to create what we in the medical business consider a sterile field. Then a large incision was made from the top of my pelvic region midsection up to four inches above my umbilicus area (belly button).

To have proper access to Seymour and the surrounding lymph nodes, they had to perform what we call an "exploratory laparotomy with right colectomy" (removal of terminal ileum, ascending colon, and proximal transverse colon—all parts of the large intestine), as well as a central mesenteric lymph node dissection along the ileocolic and right colic vessels, meticulously removing about thirty-something lymph nodes.

The terminal ileum and proximal transverse colon sites were resectioned and divided with a GIA stapler, snipping and stapling like a pro. Everything was then sealed with a device called a Ligasure, which acts like a portable Seal-a-Meal device. After everything was sealed off, they removed Seymour, performed a side-to-side ileocolic anastomosis, stapling my intestines back together with stitches to reinforce it. The last step was to rinse out my abdominal cavity with sterile water, put everything back in, and close my linea alba (the band of connective tissue that runs down the front of the abdomen) with stitches. With one last use of the surgical stapler (which resembles a small curling iron), twenty-two staples were applied to my stomach, and everything was covered with Bacitracin, gauze, and Medipore tape.

I can totally picture Dr. Sheth serving Seymour his eviction notice, like something straight out of a crime drama. "Freeze! US Marshalls. Book 'em, Danno!" and with that, he'd toss Seymour out and snap the mugshot I requested. Judging by the scowl on Seymour's face, I could tell he wasn't thrilled with the whole situation. But, oh well, he was living rent free and trying to kill me while he was there. The nerve, right? So long, my "friend."

I was fascinated with all this medical school stuff I spent years in college learning, now done on me as the patient. In layman's terms of the event: they sliced open my abdomen, removed all the cancerous guts, and sewed me back together again. End of story!

After Surgery

I must've regained consciousness sometime around 4:15 p.m. that Friday evening. I woke up in a hospital bed, groggy but alive. The nurses in the post-op unit were friendly and smiled, as most nurses do. They asked me a bunch of questions I don't remember now, but I do recall being asked about pain. They offered me Norco, which I took like a responsible patient. They also mentioned Dilaudid through an IV, available if I needed it. Well, I know enough about pain management that it's better to stay ahead of it than to wait for it to show up, so when they offered, I gladly accepted.

The more conscious I became, the more aware I was of what was going on. Seymour was gone—thank goodness—but the addict was still lurking somewhere inside of me, waiting for the right moment to pounce. I paid close attention to my pain level and kept the nurse informed. I was determined not to have pain, but I also knew better than to awaken the beast that could drag me to a park bench somewhere. As the nurses inspected my dressings to make sure no blood was seeping through, I saw the surgery site for the first time. A good six to eight inches of "track" revealed the road the knife had traveled. I spent the rest of the night in bed, resting as much as I could.

The Norco did its job, knocking me out quickly, but it came with a side effect I wasn't thrilled about: nightmares. They'd wake me up every two to three hours. Then there was the Dilaudid, which made me drowsy but didn't actually knock me out. More choices to make: stay awake and feel drowsy like I'm high, or get to sleep but have nightmares? Neither option was ideal, but the pain wasn't something I wanted to deal with either. So, I rolled with it, hoping the night would pass as quietly as possible.

Some people may not fully understand what being in recovery really entails, but I certainly do. Many relapse over decisions just like this; the temptation is right there in front of you. Opiates are no joke, and I wanted to do everything I could to avoid slipping back into that addictive dark place. I have heard of situations where people in recovery have denied the use of any opiates, but I seriously doubt you would volunteer to be cut open without them. The key is to "proceed with caution." That's the mindset I hold on to.

On day two, Saturday, Dr. Sheth came in with Seymour's mugshot post-eviction. Seymour looked *furious!* But I didn't feel an ounce of pity about showing him the door. Dr. Sheth looked at the bandages and gave a satisfied nod, saying, "Look's good." Later that day, I was surprised with my first meal in two days. Of course, it was a clear liquid diet, but since I was starving, I'd forgotten how delicious clear broth and Jell-O could be.

I feasted on that meal like Snoop Dogg mowing down a box of Fruit Loops! That was also the first day I urinated, which was exciting because everyone knows you can't leave the hospital until you can pee and have a bowel movement.

In hospital speak: they know that your elimination system is working and that peristalsis is occurring. The nurses helped me to the commode and left me to do my business in private. All I had to do was ring the bell. Life was lovely!

Healing and a New Kind of Pain

Later that night, propped up in bed and staring at Seymour's mugshot, I noticed something unusual on my doorbell camera through my phone—my roommate's car was gone. I didn't think much of it at first, but as the night went on, each time I woke from the nightmares, I checked again, and her car still wasn't there. A brief, uneasy thought crossed my mind—something wasn't right. However, the Norco meds had the answer to that, so back to sleep I went without a care on the horizon.

The next day, the good doctor came by to check on his handiwork. He removed the bandage, gave the incision a quick glance, and seemed pleased with the results. "We're just going to let it have some air from here on out," he said. Finally, I got a clear view of the twenty-two staples running down the side of my belly button—proof that I was one day closer to being discharged.

Later, while in the restroom, a small "drip" made its way from my caboose onto the floor. I was mildly embarrassed, but truly thrilled, because my body was returning to normal. I celebrated by hitting the call button to tell the nurse what had happened. She smiled and said, "No worries, sweetie, we'll clean it up for you." That was also the same day I got my first bath. Happy days are here again! I managed this on my own and scrubbed myself like I had instructed my many students when teaching bed-bath skills back at Cypress College. Things were quickly progressing, which made me smile.

With the advancement of the "caboose juice," I was upgraded to a full liquid diet: cream-of-something soup, two puddings, Jell-O, and a can of soda! Oh, it is party time now! I gulped that down like it was the best meal that has ever touched my lips! The nurse practitioner also gave the green light to discontinue my IV.

As I sat in my bed, enjoying my newfound freedom (and food), the thought of my missing roommate's car came back to me. I checked the doorbell camera again. Still no sign. Maybe she was just taking some time for herself before I came home? But when I reviewed the camera's history, that's when I saw it—she had left with her cat in its little carrier. Meds or no meds, I *knew* she had never taken the cat out before. Something was happening, but what? I felt a pain somewhere in my gut. This time it wasn't from Seymour; it wasn't physical at all. Deep and emotional, that creeping sense of abandonment seeped into my consciousness. I rang the nurse for some Norco and off to sleep I went, nightmares and all.

Sunday arrived, and I was already walking up and down the hallways on my own. I had gotten tired of being stuck in bed, and with each step, I could feel my energy returning. "When will Dr. Sheth come in to see me so I can tell him of all my progress?" I asked the nurse eagerly. She reassured me he'd be in soon. When he finally made his way to my room, he took one look at me and said, "If you keep this up—eating and passing it through—you can go home tomorrow." The rest of Sunday, I didn't ask for any pain meds. Honestly, the pain was tolerable at that point, and I didn't want them to keep me any longer. I was eager to go home.

The next day was Monday, September 2, 2024, Labor Day.

Labor Day is typically celebrated with parades, so I celebrated by marching my happiness down the hallway to the nurse's station to ask if Dr. Sheth had done his rounds yet. "Not yet," they said. I could tell they thought I was acting like one of those pesky patients wanting to get out. When the doctor arrived, he told me the good news: I was to be discharged that day. A few hours later, the nurse wheeled me out to the exit. Still somewhat drowsy, I wasn't supposed to drive myself and felt a little embarrassed that nobody was there to pick me up. But after a little convincing that I would be okay, she seemed to understand. I slowly made my way through the parking lot, across the street to where I left my car, and drove away.

Home for the Holiday

The Labor Day holiday presented a small drug problem, but thankfully, I found a pharmacy open to fill my prescription for five Norco tablets. After picking them up, I made a pit stop to grab something to eat before heading home. I stuck my key in the door, pushed it open, and stepped inside.

It was eerily quiet. Bunny—who was never out in the open because of his fear of being eaten by my roommate's pets—was perched on the dining room table near my computer, drawing my attention to a note left on the keyboard. I looked at it, then turned to Bunny. "You'd better read it, champ," he said. The note was from my roommate, telling me she had moved out. She thanked me for helping her get out of her situation, but her gift to me was my privacy back. I blinked at the note, and then at Bunny, who returned my gaze and said, "Why you looking at me? I didn't do nothing." For a moment, we both just stared at each other. "I know this wasn't your fault…" I muttered, then Bunny asked how I was doing, and I lied and said, "I'm fine."

I called Debbie just to let her know I was finally home. She wasn't happy that I was driving, but I reassured her I was done for the day.

"Is anyone there to look after you?" she asked.

"No," I said. I knew she wished she could be here to help, but as I told her I would be okay, some place inside me suddenly felt all alone. A wave of sadness flooded over me. All at once, I felt exhausted, and all I could do was lie on the couch. My cut-up gut throbbed and my heart ached. *Is this what it's like to feel abandoned?* All I wanted to do was close my eyes and make these feelings go away.

I dozed off for a bit, but the medications were wearing off, so my nap didn't last long. *My friend with breast can-*

cer would be there for me—she knows what it's like. I thought about her and wished we could have talked; I thought about my roommate. She knew I would need some help when I got home. She wasn't here, either. Again, that pain emerged, the one that wasn't coming from my wound. Then something warm dripped down my face. Sometimes crying is all a person can do in times like this. With my eyes closed, I let the chemical exchange from my tears release the oxytocin and endorphins, bringing the calm I so desperately needed. Then I did the one thing I needed more than anything else at that moment: I prayed and welcomed the temporary relief of sleep.

Eventually, I made my way upstairs. It was then I noticed the door to my roommate's room was wide open, and all her belongings, and animals, were gone. Reality has a way of feeling real and so do one's feelings.

I glanced at the pill bottle in my hand with the five Norcos in it. The pain in my abdomen seemed to intensify as I entered my bedroom. I was standing at a crossroads once again. I knew what I could do to numb it all and make it all go away.

So, I did what I knew best in times like this. I gingerly knelt on my knees and prayed. I hadn't done this since Friday morning, and welcomed the familiarity of my routine. I took only half a tablet of Norco and went to sleep. The night was mixed with interrupted slumber.

Welcome home, Anthony.

The Day After

I awoke sometime in the morning, said my prayers, and went downstairs for a cup of Folgers. It had been a while since I held Winnie and the steaming brew in my hands, and it felt great to get back into my normal routine. The mail was waiting for me, left on my table in a stack. Among it, a notice from the City of Mansfield regarding income taxes from 2022. They claimed I hadn't filed. I had called them before my surgery, explaining that I was still living and working in California during that period, so it was impossible to give them a statement proving I hadn't worked here. This letter insisted I show them proof.

I would've laughed, but that would've put pressure on my abdomen; and honestly, I kind of wanted to cry and play the "victim" card. You know, like, "Why is this all happening to me?" But the stated deadline to respond was in the next day or two, and I had heard this city would take you to court over taxes. Lord knows I had enough to deal with.

So, donning sweatpants and a ratty T-shirt as my wardrobe choice of the day, I drove myself downtown to show them my 2022 California W2s. I was secretly hoping the staples in my belly would trigger the metal detector so I could pull up my shirt, explain I had only gotten out of the hospital less than 24 hours ago, and they would feel sorry for me. However, God being God, He decided that the world wasn't ready for my nonsensical display of unwanted shenanigans, and the metal detector didn't say a word as I passed through. He also worked on the hearts and minds of the tax people, and they approved the paperwork, sparing the world my Academy Award-winning performance for the most pathetic pity party ever exhibited in Mansfield City Hall.

Since I was already out and about, feeling somewhat victorious, I figured I might as well grab a salad from my favorite spot, Swavory. I also swung by the pharmacy to pick up a few things for wound care. Exhausted from such a "full day," I called Debbie to fill her in on my adventures. She gave me a little grief, saying, "You should not be driving," and I had to agree. After hanging up with her, I looked at my discharge paperwork. Sure enough, right there it said, "No driving for at least a week." So, I called Debbie back. "You were right," I told her. She just laughed. Of course she was!

That night, I had my first real shower and took the time to carefully clean my wound. Afterward, I said my prayers and asked God to help me manage the pain. I chose not to take any Norco that night. He granted my wish—the pain was bearable, and not nearly as bad as I had expected. I sat up in bed, watching television, absentmindedly rubbing the staples along my abdomen as my mind drifted. I thought about the mission I was here to complete—Brown Manor and the nonprofit I needed to work on so solutions could be found. I traced the metal staples again—a small, tangible reminder of all that God had brought me through. I smiled and told myself that I was indeed alive. And with that, I drifted off to sleep.

Seymour

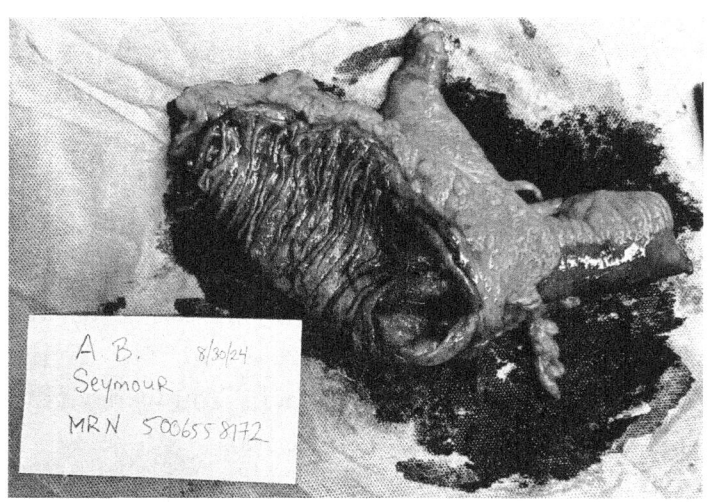

A. B.   8/30/24
Seymour
MRN 500655 8972

Chapter Fourteen
ENDINGS

The next morning brought more hopeful emotions—it felt good being in my own bed. I said a brief good morning to God as I drew my fingers down the twenty-two staples, gently touching each one, and waited for Him to answer. Life will go on, whether there is pain or not. So, slowly and with great care, I got out of bed and hit my knees just as I have done for the last twenty-five years and prayed. It always feels good to have my chit-chat with God.

I told Him of all the things I was grateful for, including the opportunity to be alive. Grateful for the bed, the comforter, the carpet I knelt on. I told Him how grateful I was to see, to breathe, to have a brain capable of linear thinking; for the water, the soap, and the towel that keeps me clean in my bathroom. And how grateful I was to have Him in my life and that He loves me.

Then I sat quietly and listened, as usual. The peace that is always available within returned. I felt its warm vibration course through my body. I knew He heard me, and all was well. I remained there—comfortably numb, for the moment—

as my fingers subconsciously traced my staples once more. And I started thinking.

The Gift

I've been given the gift of a long—though at times tumultuous—life, and as I reflect on it, I wouldn't change a thing. I entered this world with the umbilical cord wrapped around my neck—a sign, perhaps, that I was meant to fight from the start. I've fallen from windows, narrowly escaped death countless times, and sought out ways to numb myself—drinking anything I thought might help me block out reality, including rubbing alcohol, and overdosing on an assortment of drugs. I spent twenty-three years living on the streets, eating food from trash cans—a reminder of how far I had fallen. I have been such a nuisance to society that I had to be removed from the public and locked away in jails and prisons. I have isolated myself from my family, along with the rest of society, for most of my living days. At war with myself, with the world, and with everything around me, I became well-versed in hating people, places, and situations—even hating myself.

But now I see how far I've come and the lessons that even my darkest moments have taught me.

Education is truly the key to success, and the more you know, the more you grow. Over the years, I've worked in nearly every corner of healthcare, sharing in the victories of those who thought they had no chance left, celebrating their hope when they thought it was lost. I've lived on both the east and west coasts, having experienced life as both homeless and a homeowner in each. I've crossed paths with celebrities and politicians, and honestly, I can say I've called many of them my friends. I've owned sports cars, SUVs, homes, and businesses. I've traveled to many states and countries, enjoying the luxury of dining on yachts. I've befriended people from all walks of life, from the wealthiest to those who have nothing. And now, I can add something new to my list of gifts: I've survived cancer.

Yet to know God—and to know that He has accepted me, provides for me daily, and allows me to once again ask Him, "What's next?"—feels more amazing and greater than anything I can describe.

This unexpected gift hit me all at once. It wasn't until this very moment that it truly sank in. God had brought me all the way to Mansfield, Ohio, so I could discover the cancer within me, have the surgery, and face it head-on. Back then, all I knew was that He told me, "Drain your retirement accounts, pay off your house and car, and get to work on Brown Manor to help our brothers and sisters off the streets." How ironic that in my mission to save others, I ended up being saved myself. A smile crossed my face as I thought about the resistance I'd felt to follow His instructions. I can see now how God had prepared me for this moment long before I understood it. Yeah... God has a way of making things fall into place like that.

The Ghetto Practitioner

I took in a slow breath, closed my eyes, and thanked Him once again. As I sat in that moment, I felt the familiar warmth of His presence, a gentle vibration through my being. And then, I heard it, clear and steady: "Make sure your shoe-strings are tied tight, because it's time to get busy."

Getting Back to Basics

As the days passed, my wound continued healing right on schedule, and little by little, I found myself stepping back toward a "normal" life. Dr. Sheth advised me to see an oncologist and consider starting chemotherapy—to chase down any microscopic cancer cells that might still linger, waiting to grow into another Seymour. But what comes next isn't really up to me. It's God's call now. I'm tired of trying to manage everything on my own. It's time to surrender once again—to let go, and go *back to basics.*

I returned to my table and picked up my tattered red leather Bible, the one I've kept close for over two decades. It stays visible, always within reach, a constant reminder of where I've come from and the path I'm meant to stay on. As I held it, I knew it was time for a quick check-up—a heart inventory—to make sure I'm still traveling the road God set before me.

As I held the Bible in my hands, my fingers tracing its worn edges, a flood of memories from years long past washed over me. I remembered the desperate cries I once lifted to God, knowing deep down that I couldn't keep living the way I had been. I needed something far greater than myself to save me from the wreckage I had created. I remembered the moment I finally surrendered—when life had lost all meaning, and I was locked away in a prison cell, broken and empty. I could still see the image of myself carefully drying each individual garbage-soaked page of this precious book in the light that shone through my cell window. All of that seemed to mean something more to me now.

That was the first time I truly realized God was there with me. This entire transformation began with a trashcan overflowing with garbage, and why I chose to investigate it is beyond me. But there, buried and forgotten, was that soggy, discarded Bible, waiting for me to find. I felt something powerful in my hands, something I now know was His presence. From that moment on, I started journaling my thoughts, believing one day they might be shared with others, never imagining it was just the beginning of a much larger journey. As my fingers instinctively thumb through those worn, fragile pages now, I can feel that same closeness to my Creator growing stronger with every touch.

Simple but Extraordinary

Now, to all of you who have read my books, I have a confession: I don't open my Bible as often as I did when I first found it. But when I do, something beautiful still happens. The air feels fresher, the light seems brighter, and the noise of the world fades into a peaceful quiet. Life just gets a little groovier, and everything becomes a bit clearer.

With each chapter I revisit, I'm reminded of the incredible gift we've all been given—this simple, extraordinary thing called life. People sometimes ask me what the secret is, how I survived the hard things I have faced. My answer is always the same: it all started when I discovered the treasures hidden in those old, dried pages...and a whole lot of ghetto practicing. It might be hard to believe that a tiny red book, just six and a half inches tall and five inches wide, could teach me how to face my character defects and fears—and help remove them through prayer—but it did. And it still does.

Belief, like anything new, takes practice—and sometimes, if we're being honest, we're a little ghetto at it in the beginning. But that's okay. You practice it anyway. And when you see the results you were hoping for, you keep practicing it even more.

If my life has taught me anything, it's that I wasn't naturally good at much—not consistently, anyway. That's why I'm always turning back to God, always asking Him for guidance. I actually love asking Him for help in every part of my life. Practicing that connection when things are good makes it a lot easier to lean on it when things get tough. And trust me, life *will* get lifey, and I guarantee tough times will come. Life is a series of walking into the unknown.

I'm looking forward to chemotherapy and getting back to work soon. For now, I'm simply grateful—grateful to clutch my favorite morning Folgers, to chit-chat with my bestie Bunny, and to sit with my old red Bible in hand. As I flipped through its worn pages, a verse in John caught my eye: "I am the bread of life" (John 6:48), underlined long ago. I shook my head and said aloud, "Yes, God, how I know that You are!"

Us All

Before I close this book, I need to tell you something important: God loves all of us—equally and unconditionally. I couldn't have written this book without talking to Him directly. Maybe your relationship with God looks different than mine. Maybe it feels distant, or complicated, or maybe you're not even sure He's there. I get it. All I can say is this: I cannot deny what I know. God is real because I asked Him myself. And everything you've read here is part of the answer I received.

I believe He speaks to each one of us in a way that's deeply personal, in a way only we would understand. If you're willing, just ask Him. See what happens. The answers will come when you're ready to hear them. God always has our best interests at heart, even when it doesn't feel like it. And for me, it would be wrong to be disappointed with the life He's given. Everything—every heartbreak, every victory—happens in His time, not mine.

Getting to that truth? It took a lot of practice. But it's been the greatest discovery of my life.

I have learned that if I can just be still long enough and silence my brain, I can hear the gentleness of God's whispers. Writing brings His warm presence into me. Sharing these words does something completely different. What is important is that we can find meaning in the life He has so generously given to us.

So, I'll end here, still in my favorite spot at the table, holding my coffee cup with Winnie staring back at me. I take in the "best part of waking up," inhaling the steamy aroma that fills the air. I smile and call out, "Lexie, play Gordon Lightfoot," and she listens to me as "Rainy Day People" plays. I light a candle, and the scent of roses fills the room. And with a short prayer, I close my book, knowing that soon enough, another one will be opened.

Epilogue
SOME NEW BEGINNINGS

Hello again… If you are reading this, you know that *The Ghetto Practitioner* is finished, and you are holding it in your hands! But you may ask, "How are you doing now?" or "What has become of Brown Manor or what about the Foundation that you made in your mother's name? What about your recovery?"

Well, since you insist… After the surgery, the oncologist felt it best I do chemotherapy for six months, for prophylaxis purposes. I didn't want a sequel to this show, like, "The Return of Seymour," or "Seymour Takes Revenge." At first, I felt defeated by the possibility, but gave my okay, so the nurse told me about the medication and their side effects. I was emotionally numb because I have always heard unfavorable things about chemotherapy and I thought that once Dr. Sheth tossed "him" out, I was done with all of that. But I put my mind on autopilot and listened to what they said I should expect. I have no hair anyway, so alopecia wasn't a problem. Liver damage didn't sound all that fun, but when they told me the skin on my hands and feet might peel, I said, "Hold on!" As a nurse, I stand on my feet all day and, equally important, I wash my hands often. The nurse said she understood and gave me a paper with a lot more side effects listed on it.

The medications were specially ordered and were toxic. I was to take them twice a day for fourteen days, take a week off, get blood drawn to monitor things, then continue back on them on week three. They also stated it was important to eat before taking these meds. I thought, *I don't know how to cook; I am in trouble now.* I started to feel sorry for myself again—taking medications for the next six months and starving to death in a dirty house while I shed skin like a lizard! What a life: one minute living on top of the world and the next, dying alone, impersonating a smelly reptile! The only thing I could do was to turn this over to God, because I didn't know what else to do. It was time for some divine intervention. I was sure that somewhere in the side effects, it said that one day I may feel an insatiable desire to stick my tongue out and try to catch a fly.

I knew what needed to be done, so I prayed.

After spending thirty minutes with God, I felt reassured that I wouldn't turn into a lizard man, but I needed some good lotion to keep my skin moist. I also needed to get into a positive space, so I went to the church and attended a meeting. A lady named Azra agreed to help me with cleaning my house, and then I found out she could cook too! It's funny how God works. She came and helped me clean my place, cooked some wonderful gourmet meals, and taught me how to do meal preps to keep me nutritionally sound for the duration of my chemotherapy.

Weeks have passed now, and according to the oncologist, progress is being made. Relieved by this news, I am looking forward to when I no longer have to undergo chemotherapy.

Brown Manor Update

After going through several working crews, the city of Mansfield informed me permits were needed to proceed any further. When I purchased Brown Manor, it was zoned as a business, not residential. To convert it back to residential, I was told updates to the structure had to be made. I thought it would be something simple, like going down to city hall, acquiring the permits, and finding someone to do the work.

There is a saying that "more will be revealed," and I got a crash course in dealing with the zoning and permits' office. Each time I left, it was with nothing but frustration and the words, "We will contact you soon." After months of waiting, a letter arrived from the city, stating something I couldn't begin to decipher. I figured this was a good time for me to ask for help—so I did. I went to Scott, one of the board members of the foundation, and he agreed to investigate it for me. An architect named Matthew was soon brought in, and less than a month later, the city finally accepted the drawings and gave us a permit. We can now proceed from there. There is so much more to do, but I know in my heart this is a mission I was chosen for, and as long as I keep relying on that Power Greater Than Myself, all would be well.

MORE FROM THE AUTHOR

Anthony Brown

Find this book at www.AMAZON.com

or www.anthonyhowardbrown.com

ABOUT THE AUTHOR

Anthony Brown

Host of the HSBN program *I Once Had Nowhere To Go,* author, nurse practitioner, and founding director of Coordinating & Assisting Recovery Environments (C.A.R.E.), Anthony Brown knows the pain of homelessness and addiction firsthand. For 23 years, he lived on the streets, lost in despair. Today, armed with a master's degree in nursing from United States University, California, Anthony has dedicated his life to those society has forgotten. Once just a dream, Brown Manor—a long-term residential treatment home located in Mansfield, Ohio—is now becoming a reality, offering refuge for those struggling with addiction and mental illness.

His memoir, *From Park Bench to Park Avenue,* explored his redemptive journey and brought national attention to the homelessness crisis. In his follow-up, *The Ghetto Practitioner,* Anthony confronts new challenges and old strongholds, clinging to his faith and believing, "Nothing happens by mistake in God's world."

SUPPORT BROWN MANOR
The Home for the Homeless

Go to:
anthonyhowardbrown.com/brownmanor

THE JEANETTE JOAN SAFFOLD FOUNDATION (JJSF)

I smile when God gives me something to do, and before I know it, I am off doing numerous other things. The Jeanette Joan Saffold Foundation is moving along well; we're holding meetings and have a dedicated group of individuals who want to make a change within the homeless population. You can visit us at www.thejjsfoundation.org, where you can make a donation to support our nonprofit and help keep things moving forward in that area.

Life is never a straight line, and obstacles are much like pulling weeds. Persistence is needed. And that is something I know well. I will always finish what I begin; I have to. That's what God has told me to do. And since He is in charge, I move forward, beginning each task before me on my knees, in gratitude.

"Human progress is neither automatic nor inevitable... Every step toward the goal of justice requires sacrifice, suffering, and struggle; the tireless exertions and passionate concern of dedicated individuals [like you and me]."

Martin Luther King, Jr.

Please stop by if you are in Mansfield or take the virtual tour of the mansion by visiting https://anthonyhowardbrown.com/brownmanor/

Remember to always keep it groovy!

GUEST SPEAKER

Anthony Brown

www.anthonyhowardbrown.com

AUTHOR, SPEAKER, PROFESSOR

Anthony Brown is the founder and director of Coordinating & Assisting Recovery Environments (C.A.R.E.), located in Anaheim, California. Since 1999, Anthony's passion is providing specialized treatment for individuals who suffer with mental illness combined with a substance use disorder. With a master's degree in nursing from United States University, California, Anthony developed and directed a long-term residential treatment model, which has fueled his dream of opening a home for those affected by addiction and mental illness. Knowing firsthand what homelessness and addiction are like, Anthony's remarkable story offers hope and help on the journey to wholeness and recovery.

Topics:
- How to Effectively Help the Homeless
- Overcoming Childhood Trauma
- Overcoming Obstacles and Pushing Through Adversity

Event Venues:
- Conferences
- Church Services
- Seminars
- Schools
- Keynote

Book to Speak
Email: info@anthonyhowardbrown.com

If you enjoyed this book, I'd be so grateful if you'd WRITE A REVIEW….

It's easy and helps my book get into the hands of more readers.

Step 1: <u>Go To www.AMAZON.com</u>

Step 2: Search for my book in Amazon books

Step 3: Scroll down to REVIEWS

Step 4: Leave a Review

I'd love to know your thoughts about my book.

Contact me <u>info@anthonyhowardbrown.com</u>& let me know what you got out of the book.

Join my newsletter for more info on events and releases.

Sign up here: <u>www.anthonyhowardbrown.com</u>

At **Square Tree Publishing,** we believe your message matters. That is why our dedicated team of professionals is committed to bringing your literary texts and targeted curriculum to a global marketplace. We strive to make that message of the highest quality, while still maintaining your voice.

We believe in you, therefore, we provide a platform through website design, blogs, and social media campaigns to showcase your unique message. Our innovative team offers a full range of services from editing to graphic design inspired with an eye for excellence, so that your message is clearly and distinctly heard.

Whether you are a new writer needing guidance with each step of the process, or a seasoned writer, we will propel you to the next level of your development.

At Square Tree Publishing, it's all about launching YOU!

Apply TODAY to become a Square Tree author.
Go to www.squaretreepublishing.com
Click the APPLY NOW button.

Made in the USA
Middletown, DE
19 October 2025

19339133R00106